Esp

D0725568

From

Date

Daily Inspiration
for Women
from
HELEN STEINER RICE

BARBOUR BOOKS
An Imprint of Barbour Publishing, Inc.

A HELEN STEINER RICE ® Product

© 2019 by Barbour Publishing, Inc.

All poems © Helen Steiner Rice Foundation Fund, LLC, a wholly owned subsidiary of Cincinnati Museum Center. All rights reserved.

Published under license from the Helen Steiner Rice Foundation Fund, LLC.

Text compiled from Today © 1991 and This Is the Day © 1993, both compiled by Virginia J. Ruehlmann. Used with permission.

Prayers written by Janice Thompson.

ISBN 978-1-68322-727-4

All rights reserved. No part of this publication may be reproduced or transmitted for commercial purposes, except for brief quotations in printed reviews, without written permission of the publisher.

Churches and other noncommercial interests may reproduce portions of this book without the express written permission of Barbour Publishing, provided that the text does not exceed 500 words or 5 percent of the entire book, whichever is less, and that the text is not material quoted from another publisher.

When reproducing text from this book, include the following credit line: "From *Daily Inspiration for Women from Helen Steiner Rice,* published by Barbour Publishing, Inc. Used by permission."

All scripture quotations, unless otherwise indicated, are from the Revised Standard Version of the Bible, copyright 1946, 1952, and 1971 by the Division of Christian Education of the National Council of the Churches of Christ in the United States. Used by permission. All rights reserved.

Scripture quotations marked niv are taken from the Holy Bible, New International Version®. niv®. Copyright © 1973, 1978, 1984, 2011 by Biblica, Inc.™ Used by permission. All rights reserved worldwide.

Published by Barbour Books, an imprint of Barbour Publishing, Inc., 1810 Barbour Drive, Uhrichsville, Ohio 44683, www.barbourbooks.com

Our mission is to inspire the world with the life-changing message of the Bible.

 Member of the
Evangelical Christian
Publishers Association

Printed in the United States of America.

Helen Steiner Rice (1900–1981) has been called the "poet laureate of inspirational verse." The Ohio native worked as a greeting card editor before she began writing the countless inspirational poems that have been a favorite of readers for decades.

As you start this yearlong journey with the words of Helen Steiner Rice, you'll find that her beautiful verse will speak to your heart in a real and meaningful way. Read her words, meditate on scripture, and challenge yourself with devotional thoughts as you draw close to God and strengthen your relationship with Him.

Day 1

A NEW YEAR

What will you do
With this year that's so new?
The choice is yours—
God leaves that to you!

Thou crownest the year with thy bounty.
PSALM 65:11

What would you like to see come to fruition
this year? What steps can you take to
achieve those goals?

---

*Father, I'm so grateful for the opportunity to start
fresh. Each year represents a new opportunity
to begin again. I won't take it for granted,
Lord. I know I can't do it without Your help.
Guide me as I step into each new day, Lord.
Set Your plans in motion. Amen.*

Day 2

BE A LIGHT

You can't light a candle
To show others the way
Without feeling the warmth
Of that bright, little ray.

Light dawns for the righteous,
and joy for the upright in heart.
PSALM 97:11

How can you be a light of encouragement
to someone today? Who most needs
to see that light in you?

Lord, may my light shine bright for You. I want
to be known as an encourager, Father, a flame
that shines brightly, one that never goes out,
no matter how difficult life's challenges. Send me
to those who need a positive, uplifting word.
May I be a radiant reflection of You, Lord. Amen.

Day 3

SAY A LITTLE PRAYER

Games can't be won
Unless they are played,
And prayers can't be answered
Unless they are prayed.

*The sacrifice of the wicked is an
abomination to the LORD, but the
prayer of the upright is his delight.*
PROVERBS 15:8

What prayer is on your heart this week?
What is keeping you from vocalizing it to God?

---

*Father, I confess it's not always easy to share what's
on my heart. I'm afraid of being hurt.
But I can trust You, Lord. Every concern is
safe in Your holy care. So today I choose to bring
every thought, every feeling, every hurt to You.
I will not cling to them any longer, Lord.
Thank You for helping me let go. Amen.*

Day 4

GOD'S TREASURES

All of God's treasures
are yours to share
If you love Him completely
and show Him you care.

We love, because he first loved us.
1 JOHN 4:19

How have you shown God
to your neighbors lately?

Lord, I want to be a good witness for You.
May those around me never have to question
my love—for You, for them, or for others (even
people who are considerably different from me).
Guide me as I share Your love to this world.
May I be known as a generous reflection of You,
Father, one who never wavers in her faith
and never withholds her love. Amen.

Day 5

His Children

We are all God's children,
And He loves us—every one,
And completely forgives
All that we have done.

Train up a child in the way he should go,
and when he is old he will not depart from it.
PROVERBS 22:6

What guilt are you holding on to concerning
a sin that God has already forgiven?

Father, I give You permission to dig deep within
the recesses of my heart today. Take those things
that are searing my conscience, and help me
walk in Your forgiveness. Do a work in my life,
I pray, even if it's not pleasant at times.
I love and trust You, Lord! Amen.

Day 6

THE FACE OF GOD

Accept what the new year brings,
Seeing the hand of God in all things,
And as you grow in strength and grace,
The clearer you can see God's face.

*"Both riches and honor come from thee, and thou
rulest over all. In thy hand are power and might;
and in thy hand it is to make great and to
give strength to all. And now we thank thee,
our God, and praise thy glorious name."*
1 CHRONICLES 29:12–13

How has God amazed you recently?

---

*Glorious Lord! I'm amazed by Your great love,
which You pour out daily. I see Your hand every
step of the way. You give strength on days
when I'm weak and turn my sorrows into joys.
I praise You for all You are and all You're doing,
my miracle-working Father! Amen.*

Day 7

You Understand

You make me feel welcome,
You reach out Your hand,
I need never explain,
for You understand.

Welcome one another, therefore, as Christ
has welcomed you, for the glory of God.
ROMANS 15:7

How have you welcomed someone
during the past few weeks?

Lord, You've welcomed me into Your kingdom.
I'm one of the family now, with all of the glorious
kingdom benefits. How gracious You are! Show me
how to welcome others, so that they can feel the
same love You've shared so bountifully with me.
Praise You for family, Father. Amen.

Day 8

ONLY LOVE

Only love can make man kind,
And kindness of heart brings peace of mind,
And by giving love we can start this year
To lift the clouds of hate and fear.

*Jesus answered him, "If a man loves me, he will keep my
word, and my Father will love him, and we
will come to him and make our home with him."*
JOHN 14:23

Is your heart telling you to be kinder
to someone specific? If so, to whom?

---

*Father, I'll confess it's not always easy to show
kindness to everyone around me. There are
certain people (You know who they are) who
rub me the wrong way. Today I choose to
shower them with kindness, Father, even when
it's difficult. Guide me, I pray, that I might
be a true reflection of You, Lord. Amen.*

Day 9

JOY AND PEACE

Show us that in quietness
We can feel Your presence near,
Filling us with joy and peace
Throughout the coming year.

*"O my God," I say, "take me not hence in
the midst of my days, thou whose years
endure throughout all generations!"*
PSALM 102:24

How do you get focused for a talk with Jesus?

---

*My world is so noisy, Lord! I can barely hear
myself think. Take me to a quiet place where I can
be alone with You, Father. I want to draw near to
where You are, to share my heart with You and to
pour out my love, so that I might receive love in
return. What a gracious Father You are. Amen.*

Day 10

THE GREAT STORY

Show me the way, not to fortune or fame,
Not to win laurels or praise for my name. . .
But show me the way to spread the great story
That Thine is the kingdom,
the power and the glory.

*I have looked upon thee in the sanctuary,
beholding thy power and glory.*
PSALM 63:2

How often do you look for opportunities
to communicate the Gospel?

---

*Lord, my heart is wide open before You.
I'm done with seeking praise and adulation for
myself. Today I put an end to it, once and for
all. It's not about me, Lord. . .it's all about You.
I commit myself to lifting Your name before
others that they may share the abundant
life only You can give. Amen.*

Day 11

CAST YOUR CARES

No day is too dark
And no burden too great
That God in His love
Cannot penetrate.

*Be not wise in your own eyes; fear the LORD,
and turn away from evil.*
PROVERBS 3:7

How do you maintain your trust
in God when times are difficult?

---

*Even when things around me look bleak, Lord,
You are still right here beside me, shining Your
light of hope. I'm so grateful that You penetrate
the dark seasons to bear my burdens. No other
friend could offer such sweet relief, Lord.
What a loving Father You are! Amen.*

Day 12

HIS PRESENCE

May He who hears our every prayer
Keep you in His loving care—
And may you feel His presence near
Each day throughout the coming year.

The LORD is near to the brokenhearted,
and saves the crushed in spirit.
PSALM 34:18

When or where do you feel
God's presence the most?

Lord, some days I feel Your presence more than
others. I know You're right beside me, in good times
and bad. Even when I don't sense Your nearness,
Father, may I never forget that You will never leave
me or forsake me. This is a promise from Your Word.
I'm so grateful for Your nearness, Lord. Amen.

Day 13

SURRENDER

Lord, I'm unworthy, I know,
but I do love You so—
I beg You to answer my plea. . .
I've not much to give, but as long as I live,
May I give it completely to Thee!

Give heed to me, O LORD, and hearken to my plea.
JEREMIAH 18:19

When was the last time you specifically
dedicated your days to God for His use?

---

*Father, there are some days when I sense my
unworthiness more than others. I don't feel as
if I have anything to offer. Thank You for the
reminder that any worth I have comes from You.
I'm valuable in Your sight. I dedicate myself to
You today. Use me as You will, Lord. Amen.*

Day 14

MORNING PRAYER

Start every day
With a "good morning" prayer
And God will bless each thing you do
And keep you in His care.

*Every day I will bless thee, and praise thy name
for ever and ever. Great is the LORD, and greatly
to be praised, and his greatness is unsearchable.*
PSALM 145:2–3

Do you take time daily to
say good morning to God?

---

*Good morning, Lord! Thank You for this bright new
day, filled with possibilities. I look forward to seeing
what You have planned for me today, Father. Where
will I go? Who will I meet? How can I encourage
others? Lead and guide me every step of the way,
Lord, as I impact this world for You. Amen.*

Day 15

I Am Willing

Hour by hour and day by day
I talk to God and say when I pray,
"God, show me the way so I know what to do,
I am willing and ready if I just knew."

And I heard the voice of the Lord saying,
"Whom shall I send, and who will go for us?"
Then I said, "Here am I! Send me."
Isaiah 6:8

How do you best hear from God?

Lord, I'm willing and ready to follow wherever
You lead. Though I don't know where You will
send me, I trust You enough to know the journey
will be amazing. You've brought me down so
many exciting roads already, Lord, and given me
adventures at every turn. Continue to direct
my path, Father. Here I am. . .send me! Amen.

Day 16

UNCHANGING LOVE

In this changing world,
May God's unchanging love
Surround and bless you daily
In abundance from above.

But as for me, my prayer is to thee, O LORD.
At an acceptable time, O God, in the abundance
of thy steadfast love answer me.
PSALM 69:13

In what ways do you feel God's
presence during adversity?

There are times when things seem to be whirling
around me, Lord. It's hard to remain steady.
I'm close to toppling! Even during these rocky
times, Father, I sense Your presence. Though
everything around me is flipped upside down,
You are a right-side-up God. I praise You
for Your presence, Lord. Amen.

MORNING MEETING

If you meet God in the morning
And ask for guidance when you pray,
You will never in your lifetime
Face another hopeless day.

*Sing praises to the LORD, O you his saints, and give
thanks to his holy name. For his anger is but for
a moment, and his favor is for a lifetime.*
PSALM 30:4–5

In what areas do you most
frequently ask for guidance?

---

*I'm so glad You never get tired of hearing from me,
Father. Where else could I go, if not to You? I depend
on Your guidance, Lord. Others will lead me astray,
but not You. No matter what I'm facing, You point
me in the right direction. Praise You! Amen.*

Day 18

THE GIFT OF TIME

How will you use the days of this year
And the time God has placed
in your hands—
Will you waste the minutes
and squander the hours,
Leaving no prints behind in time's sands?

Behold, now is the acceptable time;
behold, now is the day of salvation.
2 CORINTHIANS 6:2

How well do you manage your time?
Are there extra minutes or hours in your
schedule when you could be working for God?

Forgive me, Lord, for wasting time. I know
our hours are limited, and I want to take full
advantage of the time You've given me to reach
others for You. Help me to see the possibilities,
Father, and give me the zeal to take that first
step so that I can impact Your kingdom. Amen.

Day 19

HEIR TO THE KINGDOM

Thank You again for Your mercy and love
And for making me heir to
Your kingdom above!

*The LORD is my strength and my shield; in him my heart
trusts; so I am helped, and my heart exults,
and with my song I give thanks to him.*
PSALM 28:7

How do you praise God?

---

*Lord, what a remarkable thought: I'm an heir to
the kingdom! Heaven is my inheritance. I can't
even fathom what it will be like, Father, but I'm
imagining grand and glorious things from the
moment I walk through those pearly gates. Even
now I praise You for the glimpse of heaven You've
placed in my heart. Thank You for placing
eternity in my heart, Father! Amen.*

Day 20

GOD IS EVERYWHERE

God's mighty hand
Can be felt every minute,
For there is nothing on earth
That God isn't in it.

*O sing to the LORD a new song, for he has done
marvelous things! His right hand and his
holy arm have gotten him victory.*
PSALM 98:1

How do you keep God in the forefront
when things are going well?

*Forgive me for getting distracted, Lord. It happens
far too frequently. You are holy and marvelous and
praiseworthy. Today I choose to put You in Your
rightful place—at the very forefront of my life.
You are worthy of my highest praise! Amen.*

THE GOLDEN CHAIN OF FRIENDSHIP

Friendship is a golden chain,
The links are friends so dear,
And like a rare and precious jewel
It's treasured more each year.

A friend loves at all times.
PROVERBS 17:17

Is God part of your closest friendships?

---

*I'm so grateful for my friends, Lord—the ones
who console me when I'm down, and the ones
who sharpen me like iron when I'm in need of
tweaking. Teach me to be the best kind of friend,
Father, one who sticks closer than a brother.
May I be a rare and precious jewel to those
I meet along life's highway. Amen.*

Day 22

STRONG FAITH

God, help me in my own small way
To somehow do something each day
To show You that I love You best
And that my faith will stand each test.

*I kept my faith, even when I said,
"I am greatly afflicted."*
PSALM 116:10

What one act of kindness has
meant the most to you?

---

*Help me not to waver, Lord! I want to stand
like a mighty oak for You. May my faith lead
the way in every decision I make and every
relationship I pursue. When things are going
well, help me to keep my focus on You. And when
I'm afflicted—when I'm hurting, Father—
show me how to keep that faith alive. Amen.*

Day 23

REST SAFELY

All who have God's blessing
Can rest safely in His care,
For He promises safe passage
On the wings of faith and prayer.

*I long to dwell in your tent forever and
take refuge in the shelter of your wings.*
PSALM 61:4 NIV

In what areas of your life do you
need to "rest safely in His care"?

---

*Lord, I'm so grateful that You choose to lead me
beside still waters. I need to separate myself from the
noise of this world and simply rest in You. Today
I choose to take refuge in You, Lord. May every
challenge, every struggle, every pain drive me to the
water's edge to spend quiet time with You. Amen.*

Day 24

BRIGHTER TOMORROWS

Whatever our problems,
our troubles and sorrows,
If we trust in the Lord,
there'll be brighter tomorrows.

I trust in the steadfast love of
God for ever and ever.
PSALM 52:8

How do you feel when you place your trust in God?

It's hard, Lord. It's hard to have faith for
tomorrow when today is already difficult
enough. I'm so relieved to know that You've
got my tomorrows taken care of. I can rest easy,
Father, because the light of Your love will
illuminate my path. Praise You, Lord! Amen.

DO TO OTHERS

Each day as it comes
brings a chance to each one
To live to the fullest,
leaving nothing undone
That would brighten the life
or lighten the load
Of some weary traveler
lost on life's road.

*Blessed be the Lord, who daily
bears us up; God is our salvation.*
PSALM 68:19

During stressful or troubling times, how difficult
is it for you to reflect God's light to others?

---

*I'll admit it, Lord—I want to be treated well,
but I don't always reciprocate the kindness of others.
You've placed me here as an ambassador to the
world, as one of Your children. May I be a reflection
of You, on good days and bad. Teach me to "do unto
others" as I would have them do unto me. Amen.*

Day 26

PRAYING FOR OTHERS

I said a little prayer for you,
and I asked the Lord above
To keep you safely in His care
and enfold you in His love.

*"If you abide in me, and my words abide in you,
ask whatever you will, and it shall be done for you."*
JOHN 15:7

How fervently do you pray for others' cares?

---

*Father, sometimes I forget that it isn't all about
me. There are others around me who are hurting.
Today I lift their needs to Your throne, Lord. Bring
healing. Bring restoration. Bring peace. Most of all,
Father, bring hope to those I love. Amen.*

Day 27

CHILDLIKE FAITH

Faith in things we cannot see
Requires a child's simplicity—
Oh, Father, grant once more
to women and men
A simple, childlike faith again.

For we walk by faith, not by sight.
2 CORINTHIANS 5:7

In what areas of your life are you
in need of a childlike faith?

---

*Lord, how trusting I was as a child! My faith was
huge. Please reactivate my childlike faith today,
Father. Restore the joy of childish simplicity so that
I can take You at Your word instead of questioning
and worrying. Thank You, Lord. Amen.*

Day 28

BURDEN LIFTER

Brighten your day
And lighten your way,
Lessen your cares
With daily prayers.

O taste and see that the LORD is good!
Happy is the man who takes refuge in him!
PSALM 34:8

What cares are holding you
back from a bright day?

Father, sometimes I feel like I'm carrying around
a heavy backpack, loaded with grief and pain that
I refuse to let go of. Today, I place that weight into
Your capable hands. Thank You for lightening my
load, Lord. Whew! I'm grateful! Amen.

Day 29

INVITE GOD

Open up your hardened heart
and let God enter in—
He only wants to help you
a new life to begin.

Don't grumble against one another, brothers and sisters,
or you will be judged. The Judge is standing at the door!
JAMES 5:9 NIV

Have you taken time to talk with God today?

Father, today I issue an open invitation for You
to enter into my heart, my situations, my woes,
my joys, my celebrations, and my heartaches.
I won't close off my heart to You, Lord. Enter,
and do a marvelous work inside and I will honor
You with praise for all You've done. Amen.

Day 30

TEACH US

Give us, through the coming year,
Quietness of mind,
Teach us to be patient
And always to be kind.

I waited patiently for the LORD;
he inclined to me and heard my cry.
PSALM 40:1

What situations try your patience?
What can you learn from these?

My patience wears thin most days, Lord. I know
You see that as You watch my comings and goings,
my reactions to things. Teach me to take a deep
breath and pause—truly, deeply pause—before
I do or say something I shouldn't. I submit
myself to the process, Lord. Amen.

Day 31

NEARLY AND DEARLY

When God forgives us,
we, too, must forgive
And resolve to do better
each day that we live
By constantly trying to be
like Him more nearly,
And trust in His wisdom
and love Him more dearly.

Bear with each other and forgive one another
if any of you has a grievance against someone.
Forgive as the Lord forgave you.
COLOSSIANS 3:13 NIV

Whom do you need to forgive?

Lord, it's hard not to hold grievances against others,
especially when they refuse to apologize or admit
they've done anything wrong. Today I choose to
forgive those who have hurt me, even the ones who
never acknowledge what they've done.
I release them. . .in Jesus' mighty name. Amen.

Day 32

PEACE

After the night, the morning,
Bidding all darkness cease,
After life's cares and sorrows,
The comfort and sweetness of peace.

*The LORD is your keeper; the LORD is your
shade on your right hand. The sun shall not
smite you by day, nor the moon by night.*
PSALM 121:5–6

What sweet times of peace have you experienced?

---

*I know what it feels like, Lord, to be knotted up
with anxiety. It happens far more times than it
should in my life. But, thanks to Your grace and
mercy, I also know what it feels like to experience
sweet release. Thank You for the peace that comes
after I turn my problems over to You, Father. Amen.*

Day 33

HOPE'S RAINBOW

We know above the dark clouds
That fill a stormy sky
Hope's rainbow will come shining through
When the clouds have drifted by.

The light of the righteous rejoices.
PROVERBS 13:9

How often do you look for a silver lining during
times of frustration?

---

*Father, I know there are brighter days coming, no
matter how dark the valley might seem. Please don't
ever let me forget that hope is a precious commodity.
No matter what else the enemy attempts to steal
from me, he can never have my hope. I refuse to
hand it over. It's Yours and Yours alone. Amen.*

Day 34

NEVER ON OUR OWN

We all have cares and problems
We cannot solve alone,
But if we go to God in prayer,
We are never on our own.

A wise man listens to advice.
PROVERBS 12:15

When have you felt Jesus by your side?

_____

*Lord, thank You for the reminder that
You are always with me. There are days when
I feel alone, but I realize You're always right
there, just a breath away. I'm so grateful for
Your presence, Father. May I never forget
that You've promised to stick with me,
no matter what I'm going through. Amen.*

Day 35

LIGHT VS. DARKNESS

God, in Thy great wisdom,
Lead us in the way that's right,
And may the darkness of this world
Be conquered by Thy light.

*"I have come as light into the world, that whoever
believes in me may not remain in darkness."*
JOHN 12:46

How is the darkness being conquered by your light?

---

*I've tried it my way so many times, Lord,
and failed every time. There's no way to
traverse a dark road on my own without
Your intervention. Today, illuminate my
path. Guide me in the direction You would
have me go. My dark days are behind me, Father.
From now on, I walk in Your light. Amen.*

Day 36

GOD WILL HELP

Let me stop complaining
About my load of care,
For God will always lighten it
When it gets too much to bear.

When the cares of my heart are many,
thy consolations cheer my soul.
PSALM 94:19

With what vices, such as
complaining, do you struggle?

I don't mean to complain when the struggles
are overwhelming, Lord, but sometimes I do.
Thank You for listening and for carrying my
burdens so that I can rest easy. Help me to turn
my whines to praise, in advance of the good
things You're sending my way. Amen.

Day 37

DAILY MIRACLES

Thank You, God, for the miracles
We are much too blind to see,
Give us new awareness
Of our many gifts from Thee.

One man pretends to be rich, yet has nothing;
another pretends to be poor, yet has great wealth.
PROVERBS 13:7

What blessings have you recognized lately?

May I never overlook Your blessings, Lord!
They are everywhere, from the moment I rise in
the morning until I fall asleep at night. Open my
eyes to see the miracles around me at every turn.
May I always be aware of Your hand at work.
I'm so grateful for each miracle, big or small. Amen.

Day 38

SYMPATHY

God enters the heart that
is broken with sorrow
As He opens the door to a brighter tomorrow,
For only through tears can we recognize
The suffering that lies in another's eyes.

_Why are you cast down, O my soul, and why are
you disquieted within me? Hope in God; for I
shall again praise him, my help and my God._
PSALM 43:5

How did you encourage someone yesterday?

_It's so easy to walk right by someone who's
hurting, Lord. I do it all the time. I'm too busy,
too distracted, to notice the pain in my loved
one's eyes. Today, point me in the direction of
one who needs a shoulder to lean on. May I be
the kind of friend You've been to me, one filled
with empathy for the hurting. Amen._

Day 39

SMALL DEEDS

Seldom do we realize
The importance of small deeds
Or to what degree of greatness
Unnoticed kindness leads.

*He stores up sound wisdom for the upright; he is a shield
to those who walk in integrity, guarding the paths of
justice and preserving the way of his saints.*
PROVERBS 2:7–8

How have you definitely had an
impact on another by being kind?

---

*Father, thank You for surrounding me with
people who care. It's the little things that warm
my heart—a phone call when I'm hurting, a text
message from someone checking in. May I never
forget that these wonderful people are reaching out
to me because I am loved. They are a beautiful
reflection of Your heart for me. Amen.*

Day 40

BRAND-NEW START

It does not take a special time
to make a brand-new start,
It only takes the deep desire
to try with all our heart.

But he who looks into the perfect law, the law of liberty,
and perseveres, being no hearer that forgets but a doer
that acts, he shall be blessed in his doing.
JAMES 1:25

What habits do you desire to change?

Lord, I confess, I have some habits that need
to go. They keep me from enjoying true freedom.
Today I ask You to revamp my desires, that
I might not crave these bad-for-me things
anymore. Thank You for second (and third
and fourth) chances, Lord. Amen.

Day 41

DAILY THANKS

No day is unmeetable
If on rising, our first thought
Is to thank God for the blessings
That His loving care has brought.

Praise the LORD! O give thanks to the LORD,
for he is good; for his steadfast love endures for ever!
PSALM 106:1

How has God been your Provider recently?

_____

I have so much to be thankful for, Lord! Your
blessings are bountiful. You've provided all I
need—physically, psychologically, and emotionally.
Your provision exceeds anything I could supply
for myself. I'm grateful beyond words, Father,
for Your loving care in my life. Amen.

Day 42

GOD IS THERE

There's no need at all
for impressive prayer,
For the minute we seek God,
He is already there!

*"Pray to your Father who is in secret; and your
Father who sees in secret will reward you."*
MATTHEW 6:6

Do your prayers border on the
impressive or the personal?

---

*I want to be real with You, Father, not repetitious
or vain. When things are falling apart in my life
(as they are prone to do), I want to bare my soul, to
share my deepest, darkest secrets and fears. Forgive
me for the times I've glossed over my prayer time
with You. Draw me close, Father. Amen.*

Day 43

LOVE IS...

Love makes us patient,
understanding, and kind,
And we judge with our hearts
and not with our minds,
For as soon as love enters
the heart's open door,
The faults we once saw are
not there anymore.

Love must be sincere.
ROMANS 12:9 NIV

Do you concentrate on others' faults?
How can you love instead?

---

*I want to have Your heart for others, Lord.
May I see them as You do—my heart filled
with compassion and love. I don't want to be
known as one who judges others but, rather, as
one who loves as You love. It's not always easy,
but it's always right. Help me, I pray. Amen.*

THE MYSTERY OF LOVE

Love can't be bought;
It is priceless and free—
Love, like pure magic,
Is a sweet mystery.

Keep your heart with all vigilance;
for from it flow the springs of life.
PROVERBS 4:23

What is the best gift of love you've ever received?

I love how You surprise me, Lord! Just when I
think no one cares, You send the perfect person
with a card, a note, a text, or a private message
on social media. You know what I need when
I need it. Thank You for surrounding me
with people who love me. Amen.

THE JOY OF LOVE

"Love one another as I have loved you,"
May seem impossible to do—
But if you will try to trust and believe,
Great are the joys that you will receive.

The wise of heart will heed commandments.
PROVERBS 10:8

How do you bring others joy by showing love?
Who in your life is more difficult to love?

Some of Your kids are tougher to love than
others, Lord. You know the ones I mean.
They make it hard at times, but I want to
keep trying. Give me Your eyes to see them
as You do, Father. I want to learn to love
even the most unlovable person. Amen.

Day 46

TELL YOUR FATHER

Remember, when you're troubled
With uncertainty and doubt,
It is best to tell your Father
What your fear is all about.

*"For I know the plans I have for you,
says the LORD, plans for welfare and not
for evil, to give you a future and a hope."*
JEREMIAH 29:11

What causes you to fear? How does
prayer help you during those times?

*Lord, sometimes I get locked up with fear.
I totally forget that I can take my worries, my
anxieties, to You. You're the One with the plans.
You're the One who knows my heart best. You've
got a great future laid out for me, Father, and I
know I can trust You. Praise You for that. Amen.*

Day 47

VISION

Take me and break me and
make me, dear God,
Just what You want me to be—
Give me the strength to
accept what You send
And eyes with the vision to see.

*But the Lord stood by me and gave me
strength to proclaim the message fully.*
2 TIMOTHY 4:17

What dreams has God given you?
Where do you think He is leading you?

---

*I can't see what's coming around the next bend,
Lord, but You can. You've placed dreams in my
heart and given me just enough vision to take
that next step forward. I trust You for what's
coming next, Father. It's going to be exciting,
filled with adventure. I can feel it. Amen.*

Day 48

EVERYWHERE MIRACLES

God's miracles
Are all around
Within our sight
And touch and sound.

Make a joyful noise to God, all the earth; sing the
glory of his name; give to him glorious praise!
PSALM 66:1–2

How do you draw joy and strength
from seeing God's work?

Father, I love the miracles that surround me—
a baby's giggle, a breathtaking sunrise, a moon that
glistens overhead, majestic mountains that point
to You. Every day I'm reminded of Your greatness,
Lord. May I never forget that each "wonder"
points straight back to You. Amen.

SELF-AWARENESS

Uncover before me my weakness and greed
And help me to search deep inside
So I may discover how easy it is
To be selfishly lost in my pride.

Pride goes before destruction,
and a haughty spirit before a fall.
PROVERBS 16:18

How can you be of service to
a neighbor or coworker today?

I'll admit it, Father—I often put my own wants
and needs above those of others. My motivations
aren't always pure. I'm self-absorbed, self-focused.
Today, Lord, I choose to lay down my pride.
I want to be a shining example of someone who
puts You first, above all, and then cares for
the needs of others. Amen.

Day 50

HE IS ENOUGH

My cross is not too heavy,
my road is not too rough,
Because God walks beside me,
and to know this is enough.

*"When you pass through the waters I will be with you;
and through the rivers, they shall not overwhelm you;
when you walk through fire you shall not be burned,
and the flame shall not consume you."*
ISAIAH 43:2

Are you walking with God as you should?
What in your life needs to change?

*Father, You are enough. I don't know why I
always feel like I'm lacking or getting the short end
of the stick. You've provided everything I need, and
You will never leave me wanting. I can trust You,
Lord. Today I choose to do just that. Amen.*

Day 51

KNEEL DOWN

God in His mercy looks down on us all,
And though what we've done
is so pitifully small,
He makes us feel welcome
to kneel down and pray
For the chance to do better
as we start a new day.

Answer me, O LORD, for thy steadfast love is good;
according to thy abundant mercy, turn to me.
PSALM 69:16

What events of yesterday would you like to revise?
With God's help, how will you start afresh today?

There's no going back, Lord, and I'm glad!
The mistakes of yesterday are embarrassing at
best. Thank You for wiping the slate clean and
giving me the opportunity to come into Your
presence once again. I'm so grateful. Amen.

Day 52

EASTER MIRACLE

Miracles are all around
Within our sight and touch and sound,
As true and wonderful today
As when the stone was rolled away.

*They were on their way to the tomb and they asked each
other, "Who will roll the stone away from the entrance of
the tomb?" But when they looked up, they saw that the
stone, which was very large, had been rolled away.*
MARK 16:2–4 NIV

What can you do to consciously remember the
resurrection in times distant from Easter?

*Father, thank You for sending Your Son to die
for my sins. What an amazing sacrifice. What a
glorious story! What a triumphant ending! How
can I ever begin to thank You for such a gift, Lord?
My heart overflows as I think about that glorious
day when Jesus rose from the grave! Amen.*

Day 53

KEEP ON SMILING

Just keep on smiling
Whatever betide you,
Secure in the knowledge
God is always beside you.

The LORD is near to all who call upon him,
to all who call upon him in truth.
PSALM 145:18

Do you find it difficult to be cheerful? How has
the Lord brought joy to your life this week?

It is only through Your power, Lord, that I'm able to
keep smiling through the rough spells. If not for Your
strength, I would surely falter. Thank You for giving
me the courage to keep going and the tenacity to face
my problems with a smile. I'm grateful. Amen.

Day 54

SOW AND HARVEST

Seed must be sown to bring forth grain,
And nothing is born without
suffering and pain.

Now he who supplies seed to the sower and bread for food
will also supply and increase your store of seed
and will enlarge the harvest of your righteousness.
2 CORINTHIANS 9:10 NIV

What good has come out of your past sufferings?

Lord, sometimes I feel like I've suffered more than
those around me. It doesn't seem balanced or fair.
Then I remember all that Your Son went through on
the cross for me, and I realize that my sufferings pale
in comparison. May I learn to see the good in every
circumstance, easy or difficult. Amen.

LOVE AND CARE

Be glad for the comfort
You've found in prayer,
Be glad for God's blessings. . .
His love and His care.

*The blessing of the LORD makes rich,
and he adds no sorrow with it.*
PROVERBS 10:22

For which of the Lord's blessings in
your life are you most thankful?

---

*I love the fact that I can turn to You when I'm
hurting, Lord. I'm also tickled to know that You're
right there, ready to celebrate with me when
blessings abound. You're an ever-present Father,
One who cares about my well-being, whether the
path is rocky or smooth. I'm so grateful. Amen.*

Day 56

FAITH TO SEE

When our lives are overcast
with trouble and with care,
Give us faith to see beyond
the dark clouds of despair.

"Therefore I tell you, do not be anxious about your life."
MATTHEW 6:25

When was the last time your faith was stretched?

---

*Lord, sometimes I feel like I'm living in a
continual state of faith-stretching. Life gives
me way too many opportunities to grow my
faith! Thank You for giving me the ability to
see beyond what I'm dealing with today. You're
growing me into a woman of faith. Amen.*

REASONS TO BE GLAD

Be glad that you've walked
with courage for each day,
Be glad you've had strength
for each step of the way,
Be glad for the comfort
you've found in prayer,
But be gladdest of all
for God's tender care.

Be glad in the LORD, and rejoice, O righteous,
and shout for joy, all you upright in heart!
PSALM 32:11

When—and why—did you
first desire to walk with Jesus?

My journey with You has been one of great joy,
Lord! From the moment I gave my heart to You,
I've had the great pleasure of spending time in
Your presence, taking my needs to Your throne,
and celebrating life's joys with Your hand in mine.
I'm grateful for Your nearness, Father! Amen.

Day 58

SERENITY

May I stand undaunted come what may,
Secure in the knowledge I have only to pray
And ask my Creator and Father above
To keep me serene in His grace and His love!

"And whatever you ask in prayer,
you will receive, if you have faith."
MATTHEW 21:22

How much and how often
do you pray during adversity?

Lord, sometimes I forget that I can rest easy once
I've delivered my prayer requests to Your throne.
I can give up on fretting because You've got
my best interest at heart. When troubles come,
may I never forget that You are my final
stop, Father. You've got this. Amen.

Day 59

WAIT

If when you ask for something
And God seems to hesitate,
Never be discouraged—
He is asking you to wait.

May integrity and uprightness preserve me,
for I wait for thee.
PSALM 25:21

Why might God be asking you to
wait for something you desire?

Waiting is not my strong suit, Father. I get
impatient at times. I'm reminded today that
seasons of waiting can be seasons of great
growth, development, and healing. I choose
to be encouraged as I wait on You, Lord.
Thank You for the work You are doing in
my life, no matter how long it takes. Amen.

Day 60

BETTER TOMORROW

God, be my resting place and my protection
In hours of trouble, defeat, and dejection,
May I never give way to self-pity and sorrow,
May I always be sure of a better tomorrow.

*Every word of God proves true; he is a
shield to those who take refuge in him.*
PROVERBS 30:5

When have you given in to self-pity—
and how did you defeat that kind of thinking?

---

*I'll admit it, Lord: I often feel sorry for
myself. I think my problems are bigger than
the ones my friends and loved ones face. I get
down in the dumps. I give up. Thank You for
the reminder that tomorrow will be better
than today. What a Hope-Giver You are! I'm
so grateful for Your reassurance, Lord. Amen.*

Day 61

Spring Awakening

Flowers sleeping peacefully
beneath the winter's snow
Awaken from their icy grave when
spring winds start to blow.

*So we do not lose heart. Though our outer
nature is wasting away, our inner
nature is being renewed every day.*
2 Corinthians 4:16

What untapped potential, forgotten dreams,
or unused talents are lying dormant within you?

---

*I feel a new day dawning, Lord! New things are
springing forth, and I'm so excited. Take every
dream, every gift, every talent, and show me how
to make an impact on the kingdom of God. Use me,
Father, to reawaken dreams in others, I pray. Amen.*

Day 62

NEW LIFE

The bleakness of the winter
is melted by the sun,
The tree that looked so stark
and dead becomes a living one.

*Water will gush forth in the wilderness
and streams in the desert.*
ISAIAH 35:6 NIV

Has unforgiveness taken root in your heart,
preventing you from being an example of Christ?

---

*Father, help me to forgive, even those who've
harmed me the most. I don't want my heart to
grow cold. I want streams in the desert, Father.
That can only happen if I release those who've
wounded me. Today I choose to do that, Lord,
but I need Your help to let go. Amen.*

Day 63

UNKNOWN FRIENDS

Widen the vision of my unseeing eyes,
So in passing faces I'll recognize
Not just a stranger, unloved and unknown,
But a friend with a heart that is
much like my own.

Then turning to the disciples he said privately,
"Blessed are the eyes which see what you see!
For I tell you that many prophets and kings
desired to see what you see, and did not see it."
LUKE 10:23–24

Are you quick to judge others? How can you keep
an open heart and seek the truth instead?

I crave friendship, Lord. Help me not to push
others away by judging or expecting too much.
I want to be a real friend, one who sticks closer
than a brother. Soften my heart and help
me see others the way You see them, Father.
Keep my heart wide open, I pray. Amen.

LOVE ONE ANOTHER

Love works in ways that are
wondrous and strange,
And there is nothing in life
that love cannot change,
And all that God promised
will someday come true
When you love one another
the way He loved you.

"As the Father has loved me, so have I loved you.
Now remain in my love. If you keep my commands, you
will remain in my love, just as I have kept my Father's
commands and remain in his love."
JOHN 15:9–10 NIV

Which of God's promises are you eagerly awaiting?

Father, I love the words to this poem because they
remind me that You're a promise keeper. If You
said it, it will come to pass. I don't have to fret or
wonder "if." I just have to trust that You know
the "when." Thank You for the reminder, Lord.
I can't wait to see what You have in store. Amen.

Day 65

MEDITATE ON HIM

To understand God's greatness
And to use His gifts each day
The soul must learn to meet Him
In a meditative way.

To get wisdom is better than gold; to get
understanding is to be chosen rather than silver.
PROVERBS 16:16

When do you like to spend time
with God and read His Word?

Father, I love to meditate on Your Word—
to take scriptures and plant them deep in my
heart, to ponder them, to eat them as one would
eat food. When I really take the time to meditate
on Your Word, Your goodness, Your love, I am
transformed, Lord. Thank You for changing
me as I spend time with You. Amen.

Day 66

FAITH AND LOVE AND PRAYER

There can be no crown of stars
Without a cross to bear,
And there is no salvation
Without faith and love and prayer.

Blessings are on the head of the righteous.
PROVERBS 10:6

What is your "cross" to bear? How can you reflect the
grace and glory of God through this time?

---

*Lord, when I look at the things that weigh me
down, the crosses I must bear, I get overwhelmed.
Thank You for the reminder that You will never
give me more than I can withstand. There will
be a crown of stars and blessings in abundance
as I persevere. Praise You, Father. Amen.*

TRUST AND FOLLOW

There are many things in life
That we cannot understand,
But we must trust God's judgment
And be guided by His hand.

The LORD is a stronghold to him whose way is upright.
PROVERBS 10:29

Are you asking for God's guidance every day,
in every way? In which situations are
you trusting Him to lead you?

---

*Father, I so often want to step out on my own,
to forge my own trail. Today I ask for Your
guidance. I submit myself to the process of
following and not leading. I trust You, Lord,
even when I can't see what's coming around
the next bend. Praise You! Amen.*

WHAT IS HAPPINESS?

Happiness is giving up wishing
for things we have not
And making the best of
whatever we've got—
It's knowing that life is determined for us
And pursuing our tasks without
fret, fume, or fuss.

*There is great gain in godliness with contentment;
for we brought nothing into the world,
and we cannot take anything out of the world.*
1 TIMOTHY 6:6–7

Are you living a contented life—
or a cantankerous one?

---

*Father, it's hard to admit this, but I've often
used the words "I'll be happy. . .when." When
the bank account is full. When I'm in perfect
health. When I'm at my target weight. When
all of my relationships are perfect. Today I
choose Your version of happiness, Father. I
choose contentment. Though my circumstances
might not change, I choose to do so. Amen.*

Day 69

GOD'S MERCY

Let us face the trouble that is
ours this present minute,
And count on God to help us
and to put His mercy in it.

The Lord disciplines the one he loves.
HEBREWS 12:6 NIV

Are you good at asking for help?
Are you better at giving help?

---

*Facing trouble isn't always easy for me, Lord.
I often feel like I won't have what it takes to
face the challenge. Thank You for the reminder
that Your mercy will see me through. I need
Your help in so many areas of my life, Father.
I'm grateful for the help You provide, even when
I don't realize just how badly I need it. Amen.*

Day 70

THE FATHER'S CREATION

Our Father made the heavens,
The mountains and the hills,
The rivers and the oceans,
And the singing whippoorwills.

Let them praise the name of the LORD! For he
commanded and they were created. And he
established them for ever and ever; he fixed
their bounds which cannot be passed.
PSALM 148:5–6

What aspects of nature speak to you?
How do they affect you?

Oh, how I love Your creation, Lord! All around me,
nature sings Your praises. My heart comes alive in
the great outdoors as I drink in Your vast creative
greatness. From the mightiest mountain to the
tiniest creature, I thank You for them all, Lord.
All of nature points to You. Amen.

Day 71

LIFE'S SOJOURN

Enjoy your sojourn on earth and be glad
That God gives you a choice
between good things and bad,
And only be sure that you heed God's voice
Whenever life asks you to make a choice.

"Today, if you hear his voice,
do not harden your hearts."
HEBREWS 3:7–8 NIV

How has God shown you the right path?

_____

I'll keep walking with You, Lord. I've tried
to head off in my own direction and found
myself lost. Floundering. My ear is tuned in
to Your voice, Father. I'm listening for Your
instructions. Turn to the right, You say?
That's exactly what I'll do. Every day of
my life I commit to follow You. Amen.

Day 72

YOUR NAME IS INCLUDED

God's love knows no exceptions,
So never feel excluded—
No matter who or what you are,
Your name has been included.

Let your face shine on your servant;
save me in your unfailing love.
PSALM 31:16 NIV

Can you brighten someone's day by including him or
her in an upcoming activity?

It feels so good to be included, Lord—not just
by You, but Your people. I love to be part of the
family, one of Your kids. From this day forth,
show me how to reach out to others so that they
can feel this sense of inclusion too. I will do my
best to usher people into the group so that none
are ever alone. Thank You for reminding
me how much this matters to You. Amen.

Day 73

WINNING LIFE'S BATTLES

Most of the battles
of life are won
By looking beyond the clouds
to the sun.

On the day I called, thou didst answer me,
my strength of soul thou didst increase.
PSALM 138:3

Are you in the practice of
looking to the Son for answers?

I get weary with fighting, Lord. It seems like
life is just one battle after another. Thank You
for the reminder that it's Your strength I'm
needing, not my own. You're the One who's
fighting my battles for me, Lord. I can rest
easy in You. I'm so grateful! Amen.

Day 74

MAKE NEW FRIENDS

May we try
In our small way
To make new friends
From day to day.

A faithful envoy brings healing.
PROVERBS 13:17

Are you holding on to some burdens
that you could give to God?

---

*Father, I'm so grateful for the friends You've
placed in my path. They are faithful companions,
willing to listen to my woes and pray when
I'm down. Best of all, they bring joy and laughter
into my life. May I be the kind of friend to them
that they have been to me, Lord. Amen.*

Day 75

LIVE TODAY

Forget the past and future
And dwell wholly on today,
For God controls the future,
And He will direct our way.

A future awaits those who seek peace.
PSALM 37:37 NIV

What are you looking forward to today? . . .
Tomorrow? . . .

I need the reminder to live in the moment,
Lord. Sometimes I get bound up by the things
of the past. They tighten around me like a noose.
Today I release them back to You. May I truly
let go of yesterday and embrace today so that I
can step into a more hopeful tomorrow. Amen.

Day 76

COUNT YOUR BLESSINGS

Happiness is waking up
And beginning the day
By counting our blessings
And kneeling to pray.

Happy the people to whom such blessings fall!
Happy the people whose God is the LORD!
PSALM 144:15

How many ways have you been blessed today?

Lord, You've blessed me in immeasurable ways.
Sometimes I forget to pause and thank You for
Your many gifts. I'm so grateful, Father, for
Your provision, Your love, Your companionship.
May I never forget that every good and perfect
gift comes from You and You alone. Amen.

Day 77

THE RISEN SAVIOR

In the resurrection
That takes place in nature's sod,
Let us understand more fully
The risen Savior, Son of God.

*Rise up, come to our help! Deliver us
for the sake of thy steadfast love!*
PSALM 44:26

What part of the Resurrection story
means the most to you and why?

---

*"I serve a risen Savior!" Oh, how I love
those words, Lord. What a remarkable end to
the redemption story. Your Son came bursting
forth from the grave, a sign to all that death
has no victory over us. May I choose to walk
in that resurrection power, not just today,
but every day of my life. Amen.*

Day 78

GOD UNDERSTANDS

No matter what your past has been,
Trust God to understand,
And no matter what your problem is,
Just place it in His hand.

"Forget the former things; do not dwell on the past."
ISAIAH 43:18 NIV

In what ways do you want to be more like Jesus?

---

*You get it, Lord. You understand. When
no one else seems to comprehend what I'm
going through, You "get" the intricacies of
my situation, and (best of all) You care about
how I feel. It helps so much to know that I'm
not alone, that You are right here, fully aware
and filled with compassion, Father. Amen.*

Day 79

A New Day

I see the dew glisten in crystal-like splendor
While God, with a touch that
is gentle and tender,
Wraps up the night and softly tucks it away
And hangs out the sun to herald a new day.

*The sun shall not smite you by day,
nor the moon by night.*
Psalm 121:6

When was the last time you watched a sunrise?

Some days seem to drag on forever, Lord, while others pass in the blink of an eye. Many I'd like to forget. Others, I'd love to remember forever. Today I thank You for the gift of a new day, where all things are made new. May I never forget that each one is a present from You, Father. Amen.

Through God's Eyes

When we view our problems
through the eyes of God above,
Misfortunes turn to blessings,
and hatred turns to love.

*"You will seek me and find me when
you seek me with all your heart."*
Jeremiah 29:13 niv

What do you suppose God
thinks about your problems?

---

*Oh, how I wish I had Your vision, Lord. To see
things the way You see them would certainly put
my woes in perspective. Your view is elongated.
You see not only what I'm walking through today
but where it's leading me tomorrow. . .and all
the days beyond. I trust You, Father. Amen.*

Day 81

HIS PRESENCE IS NEAR

God's presence is ever beside you,
As near as the reach of your hand,
You have but to tell Him your troubles,
There is nothing He won't understand.

Thou dost show me the path of life; in thy
presence there is fulness of joy, in thy right
hand are pleasures for evermore.
PSALM 16:11

Is God your first resource for help—or your last?

I know I can't depend on feelings, Father, but there's
something about sensing Your nearness that brings
such comfort, especially when I'm walking through
a valley. Thank You for sticking close, for not
abandoning me, even when I stumble off the beaten
path. What a faithful Friend You are, Lord. Amen.

Day 82

ETERNAL SPRING

Man, like flowers, too must sleep
Until he is called from the darkest deep
To live in that place where angels sing
And where there is eternal spring!

*"For the hour is coming when all who are in
the tombs will hear his voice and come forth."*
JOHN 5:28–29

What are you looking forward to in heaven?

*There's coming a day, Lord—and I'm looking
forward to it—when You're going to call my name
and take me to heaven to live forever with You.
I have no fear as I ponder that day, only excitement
for the joys of eternity. May I set my sights on the
eternal, Lord, not the temporary. Amen.*

Day 83

NO FEAR

Little brooks and singing streams,
icebound beneath the snow,
Begin to babble merrily beneath
the sun's warm glow,
And all around on every side
new life and joy appear
To tell us nothing ever dies
and we should have no fear.

*For this slight momentary affliction is preparing for us an
eternal weight of glory beyond all comparison.*
2 CORINTHIANS 4:17

How has your attitude been lately? Are you positively
affecting others or freezing friendships?

---

*I know what it's like to be gripped with fear,
Lord; and I know what it's like to release
those fears to You. There are "slight momentary
affliction[s]" that distract me (and bring pain
and fear), but they are nothing in light of eternity.
May I keep my focus on You, so that I can see
every situation through eternal eyes. Amen.*

Day 84

THE RISEN SAVIOR

Shed Thy light upon us as
Easter dawns this year,
And may we feel the presence
of the risen Savior near.

"The Lord has risen indeed."
LUKE 24:34

When did Easter first hold
spiritual meaning for you?

It's the dawning of a new day, Lord—
a brand-new life, thanks to Your resurrected Son.
I sense so many new things coming, Father—
new possibilities, new joys, new relationships.
I'm so grateful for Your light, which shines in
darkness and guides my way as I step out onto
the path toward this new life. Amen.

GRANT US GRACE

God, grant us grace to use
all the hours of our days
Not for our selfish interests
and our own willful ways.

*And he came to the disciples and found them
sleeping; and he said to Peter, "So, could
you not watch with me one hour?"*
MATTHEW 26:40

How often are you self-serving?

---

*Today I choose to turn my eyes upon You, Lord,
not myself. I don't want to be self-serving, Father.
No more focusing on my own issues, my own
concerns. May my eyes remain open and fixed
on You, no matter what I'm walking through.
Guide me every step of the way, Father. Amen.*

LIFE'S LOVELY GARDEN

Life's lovely garden would
be sweeter by far
If all who passed through it
were as nice as you are.

*"For lo, the winter is past, the rain is over
and gone. The flowers appear on the earth,
the time of singing has come, and the voice
of the turtledove is heard in our land."*
SONG OF SOLOMON 2:11–12

Do you need to reconnect with a friend
or tell one how much she means to you?

---

*How precious, this garden of friends, Lord!
They are like flowers to my soul, alive with
beauty and fragrance, bringing such joy to my life.
I thank You for every single one—the ones who
bloom with great color and the ones who prefer
to stand quietly among the others. Amen.*

Day 87

WE LIVE AGAIN

Our Savior's resurrection was
God's way of telling men
That in Christ we are eternal
and in Him we live again.

*"For this is the will of my Father, that every one who
sees the Son and believes in him should have eternal life;
and I will raise him up at the last day."*
JOHN 6:40

Have you thanked God for His
eternal salvation and grace lately?

---

*The idea of coming alive again after death is
so amazing, Lord! To spring to life once more,
defeating the grave? A remarkable notion! That's
what You had in mind all along when You sent
Your Son with His mighty resurrection power!
I can hardly wait to witness that resurrection
power firsthand, Father. Amen.*

Day 88

HIS WILL

God only answers our pleadings
When He knows that our wants fill a need,
And whenever our will becomes His will,
There is no prayer that God does not heed!

"The LORD will guide you always;
he will satisfy your needs."
ISAIAH 58:11 NIV

Is your will in line with God's
about the things you desire?

Father, when I pray, "Your will be done,"
I'm saying that I submit my wants, wishes,
and desires to Your greater plan. I'm coming into
alignment with Your best for my life. Nothing I
could ever come up with on my own will even
come close, Lord. Today, with everything in me,
I cry, "Your will, not mine." Amen.

Day 89

SPRING'S ARRIVAL

The sleeping earth awakens,
the robins start to sing,
The flowers open wide their eyes
to tell us it is spring.

*"Why is it thought incredible by any
of you that God raises the dead?"*
ACTS 26:8

What about spring makes you joyful?

---

*How I love the springtime, Lord, when all
sleeping things awaken. What hope it brings
to see those colors burst forth. I'm so grateful
for the springtime. Thank You for renewing
and regenerating all things, Father. Amen.*

Day 90

A New Season

Flowers sleeping 'neath the snow,
Awakening when the spring winds blow,
Leafless trees so bare before
Are gowned in lacy green once more.

Like the crocus, it will burst into bloom;
it will rejoice greatly and shout for joy.
ISAIAH 35:1–2 NIV

What makes you "burst into bloom"?

Father, there are dreams and desires, hopes and
wishes planted deep in my heart. Sometimes I
feel like it's "forever winter" and that my time
will never come. Thank You for the reminder
that spring is on its way. You care about my
dreams, Lord, and will bring to life those
things that please Your heart. Amen.

Day 91

CREATION SPEAKS

Sometimes when faith is running low
And I cannot fathom why things are so,
I walk among the flowers I grow
And learn the answers to all I would know.

As you have heard from the beginning,
his command is that you walk in love.
2 JOHN 1:6 NIV

How do you relax and hear God speaking to you?

You speak to me in so many ways, Lord. All of
creation sings Your praises. The birds, the rustling
leaves of the trees, the early morning breeze—all
of these things point to You and remind me of Your
creative hand at work all around me. Thank You for
speaking through Your creation, Father. Amen.

Day 92

RENEW ME

You are ushering in another day,
Untouched and freshly new,
So here I come to ask You, God,
If You'll renew me, too.

Create in me a clean heart, O God, and
put a new and right spirit within me.
PSALM 51:10

When did you last feel fully
refreshed and renewed spiritually?

Brand-new. That's how this day feels, Father.
It's a new chance to get things right, another
opportunity to spend time with You, and a clean
slate, ready to be filled with wonders anew.
Thanks for pushing the REFRESH button,
Lord. I needed this brand-new day. Amen.

Day 93

GOODNIGHT

Who but God
Could make the day
And softly put
The night away?

*Thine is the day, thine also the night; thou hast
established the luminaries and the sun.*
PSALM 74:16

Are you a morning person or a night owl? What
positive things can you find about the opposite time?

---

*The sun rises and sets according to Your Word,
Lord. What a remarkable miracle to watch
that shimmering ball of light illuminate a
brand-new day. Every morning it peeks
through, ready to cast its golden rays so that I
can experience new hopes, new possibilities.
Thank You for lighting my way, Father. Amen.*

Day 94

APRIL

April comes with cheeks a-glowing,
Flowers bloom and streams are flowing,
And the earth in glad surprise
Opens wide its springtime eyes.

Be exalted, O God, above the heavens;
let your glory be over all the earth.
PSALM 108:5 NIV

When has someone brought joy
and happiness into your life?

All of the earth cries out to You, Father. Majestic
mountain peaks, flowing rivers, trickling streams,
whippoorwills and cicadas. . .all join a masterful
chorus, a symphony of praise to remind us that
the earth is excited to spring to life once again.
How majestic You are, Father! Amen.

Day 95

LAY IT DOWN

We never meet our problems alone,
For God is our Father and we are His own,
There's no circumstance we cannot meet
If we lay our burden at Jesus' feet.

He raises up the needy out of affliction.
PSALM 107:41

How has Jesus revealed Himself
to you in previous times of need?

*Sometimes I feel so needy, Lord. I'm like a child,
arms extended, crying out for her mother to make
everything right. I'm so grateful You're close by,
Father, ready to take these burdens from me. Today
I cast them at Your feet, readily admitting that
I cannot fix things on my own. Thank You for
caring so deeply about my needs, Lord. Amen.*

GOD IS LOVE

No one is a stranger in God's sight,
For God is love, and in His light
May we, too, try in our small way
To make new friends from day to day.

*"Then the King will say to those at his right hand,
'Come, O blessed of my Father, inherit the kingdom
prepared for you from the foundation of the world;
for I was hungry and you gave me food, I was
thirsty and you gave me drink, I was a
stranger and you welcomed me.'"*
MATTHEW 25:34–35

How can you reach out and
be a blessing this week?

---

*There are no strangers in Your family, Lord.
We're all included, all loved, all equal. You look
down on Your kids with equal tenderness, equal
opportunity, equal joy. Thank You for the reminder
that this is a "Come one, come all" community
You've placed me in. I'm so grateful for my
brothers and sisters in Christ. Amen.*

Day 97

GOD'S GREAT LOVE

Keep us gently humble in
the greatness of Thy love,
So someday we are fit to dwell
with Thee in peace above.

*And he said to the woman,
"Your faith has saved you; go in peace."*
LUKE 7:50

Do you struggle with pride? How is the
Lord helping you with this weakness?

---

*I must confess: pride has been a problem at times,
Lord. I get a little puffed up and impressed by
my own abilities. Thank You for the reminder
that all things come from You. Apart from You,
I have no abilities at all! May my focus forever
remain fixed on the One who empowers me
and fits me for the work ahead. Amen.*

Day 98

RISE ABOVE

Like a soaring eagle
You, too, can rise above
The storms of life around you
On the wings of prayer and love.

*"Therefore I tell you, whatever you ask in prayer,
believe that you have received it, and it will be yours."*
MARK 11:24

When have you felt surrounded by prayer?
How has knowing that helped the situation?

*Father, I needed the reminder that I can soar above
my circumstances. Sometimes I get bogged down, as
if my feet were in quicksand. I look at the problems,
not at You. I'm so grateful when You take me by the
hand and set my heart to flight, Lord. How freeing,
to soar above and beyond those pesky things that
threaten to weigh me down. I'm so grateful. Amen.*

Honor and Truth

Give us strength and courage
to be honorable and true,
Practicing Your precepts
in everything we do.

*Finally, brethren, whatever is true, whatever is
honorable, whatever is just, whatever is pure,
whatever is lovely, whatever is gracious, if there
is any excellence, if there is anything worthy of
praise, think about these things. What you have
learned and received and heard and seen in me,
do; and the God of peace will be with you.*
Philippians 4:8–9

When do you find it difficult
to adhere to God's laws?

---

*Thank You for Your precepts, Father. Your
Word is full of guidelines for my life. I'm so glad
You've taken Your laws and imprinted them on
my heart, so that I might not sin against You, Lord.
I obey out of love, not fear. What an amazing
opportunity to show my love on a daily basis.
Thank You for Your guidance. Amen.*

Day 100

A Rich Harvest

Rejoice though your heart is broken in two,
God seeks to bring forth a rich harvest in you.

*"While the earth remains, seedtime and harvest, cold and
heat, summer and winter, day and night, shall not cease."*
Genesis 8:22

What areas of your life might God be harvesting?

_____

*Not every day feels like a celebration, Lord. Some
days I can barely lift my head, let alone shout praises.
But I'm learning, Father. I'm discovering that,
even when my heart is broken, even when areas of
my life are in harvest season, praise is still the best
way to power through any situation. Amen.*

Day 101

A MOTHER'S LOVE

A mother's love is fashioned
After God's enduring love,
It is endless and unfailing
Like the love of Him above.

Serve one another humbly in love.
GALATIANS 5:13 NIV

How does your mother reflect
God's character of love?

---

*Father, I don't thank You often enough for my
mother and the other motherly figures You've
placed in my life. What a blessing to know
women who exemplify Your love, Your goodness,
Your grace. May I become that kind of woman
as I walk this road with You. Amen.*

INFINITE BLESSINGS

No matter how big man's dreams are,
God's blessings are infinitely more,
For always God's giving is greater
Than what man is asking for.

*He will receive blessing from the LORD,
and vindication from the God of his salvation.*
PSALM 24:5

Which of God's gifts to you were
greater than what you asked for?

---

*I'll admit it, Lord—I don't always see blessings
as the gift they are. The breath in my lungs.
The sun shining overhead. A warm house to sleep
in. These seem so ordinary, so commonplace to
me. But these and a million other blessings are
straight from Your hand, and all because of Your
vast love for me. Praise You, Father! Amen.*

Day 103

HEART GIFTS

It's not the things that can be bought
That are life's richest treasure,
It's just the little heart gifts
That money cannot measure.

*"Give, and it will be given to you. A good measure,
pressed down, shaken together and running over,
will be poured into your lap. For with the measure
you use, it will be measured to you."*
LUKE 6:38 NIV

What "heart gifts" can you give someone today?

---

*What a treasure trove, Lord—the gifts I've received
over the years. Handmade cards, pictures colored
by children, trinkets and treasures aplenty. May I
never overlook the value in these precious heart gifts.
Each one represents a person expressing love straight
from the heart. I'm so grateful, Father. Amen.*

Day 104

MEET EACH DAY

Some work to do, a goal to win,
A hidden longing deep within
That spurs us on to bigger things
And helps us meet what each day brings.

*Let us run with perseverance
the race that is set before us.*
HEBREWS 12:1

Toward what goal are you persevering?

---

*Father, as I point myself in the direction of the
goals I've set, take my hand. Guide me. Show me
the steps to take, not just today, but all the days
hereafter. I've got work to do, Lord; but I know
that, with Your help, I can be successful. Today
I choose to persevere, no matter how tough.
We'll get this done, Father! Amen.*

BLOOMS OF FRIENDSHIP

Friendship, like flowers,
blooms ever more fair
When carefully tended
by dear friends who care.

*"Their life shall be like a watered garden,
and they shall languish no more."*
JEREMIAH 31:12

What friendships do you see blooming this year?

---

*Lord, I'm so grateful for the friends who've
been in my life for so many years, but I'm equally
grateful for the newer/blossoming ones. What
an unexpected delight, to see new friendships
growing, seemingly from out of nowhere. I know
You orchestrated it all, Father, for You are the
great Gardener. Praise You. Amen.*

Day 106

DIVINE GUIDANCE

When we cut ourselves away
from guidance that's divine,
Our lives will be as fruitless
as the branch without the vine.

*"I am the true vine, and my Father is the vinedresser.
Every branch of mine that bears no fruit, he takes away,
and every branch that does bear fruit
he prunes, that it may bear more fruit."*
JOHN 15:1–2

What fruit has come from
God's pruning of your life?

---

*I don't ever want to separate myself from You,
Father. You're the Source of all life. I want to thrive,
to flourish, to remain in You, that I might become
a fruit bearer. Even during the pruning seasons,
may I remain close, linked forever to Your heart,
Lord. I praise You for being my all in all. Amen.*

MANY BLESSINGS

The good, green earth beneath our feet,
The air we breathe, the food we eat—
All these things and many more
Are things we should be thankful for.

"As the heavens are higher than the earth, so are
my ways higher than your ways and my thoughts
than your thoughts. As the rain and the snow come
down from heaven, and do not return to it without
watering the earth and making it bud and flourish,
so that it yields seed for the sower and bread for the eater,
so is my word that goes out from my mouth."
ISAIAH 55:9–11 NIV

How do you show your appreciation
to God for His blessings?

Have I said "Thank You" lately, Lord? For the
grass under my feet? My place of employment?
The car I drive? The people You've surrounded
me with? Have I thanked You for the food I
eat, the paycheck I cash, the neighbors I visit?
When I break it down, when I count the
blessings one by one, I'm simply overwhelmed
by Your loving care for me. Thank You! Amen.

Day 108

HE IS ARISEN

He was crucified and buried
but today the whole world knows
The Resurrection story
of how Jesus Christ arose.

They got up and returned at once to Jerusalem.
There they found the Eleven and those with them,
assembled together and saying, "It is true!
The Lord has risen and has appeared to Simon."
LUKE 24:33–34 NIV

How would you have felt as one of
Jesus' disciples after the resurrection?

I can't even imagine how it must have felt,
Lord, to see that empty tomb! What a shock,
and what confirmation that the story would
have a far better ending than they had feared.
I'm so grateful for Your resurrection power,
Father! It emboldens me, challenges me, and
serves as a constant reminder that You are above
and beyond all I could ever ask or think.
You are worthy to be praised, Lord! Amen!

CHANGES

After the clouds, the sunshine,
After the winter, the spring,
After the shower, the rainbow—
For life is a changeable thing.

The LORD is my light and my salvation;
whom shall I fear?
PSALM 27:1

How is your life changing right now?
Are you accepting this change or fighting it?

There are "afters" coming in my life, Lord. I can
feel them. After pain. . .joy. After loss. . .restitution.
After heartache. . .peace. You never leave us in a
"before/during" state, and I'm so very grateful.
What the enemy means for evil in my life You can
(and do) use for good. How grateful I am for all
of the "afters" yet to come. Praise You! Amen.

DIVINE RENEWAL

After the winter comes the spring
To show us again that in everything
There's always renewal, divinely planned,
Flawlessly perfect, the work of God's hand.

For the LORD is a great God. . . . In his hand
are the depths of the earth; the heights
of the mountains are his also.
PSALM 95:3–4

What might God be renewing in you today?

Father, how I love the prefix "re-." You're renewing,
reviving, restoring, reinventing, and so much more.
May I never lose sight of this prefix in my life,
even in the middle of the battles I face. There's a
"re-" coming around the bend, no matter what
things look like in the moment. I'm so grateful
for Your renewal, Lord! Amen.

SUN AND SHOWERS

God, give us wider vision to
see and understand
That both the sun and showers
are gifts from Thy great hand.

*So if you faithfully obey the commands I am giving
you today—to love the LORD your God and to serve him
with all your heart and with all your soul—
then I will send rain on your land in its season, both
autumn and spring rains, so that you may gather
in your grain, new wine and olive oil.*
DEUTERONOMY 11:13–14 NIV

How do you adjust to God's unexpected
or unwelcome gifts?

---

*Father, I want my life to be rosy at every turn,
for problems to tuck themselves away, far out of
sight and mind. But I'm learning, Lord, that
even the hardest of times, the deepest of woes,
can turn out to be blessings in the end. You can—
and do—take life's challenges and sharpen me
with them, growing me into a woman of
strength. I don't always love the growth seasons,
but I'm so happy to be strong in You. Amen.*

Day 112

FOREVER YOURS

Kings and kingdoms all pass away,
Nothing on earth endures,
But the love of God who sent His Son
Is forever and ever yours.

But thou, O LORD, art enthroned for ever;
thy name endures to all generations.
PSALM 102:12

How has knowing God's unchanging and
constant love made a difference in your life?

It seems like nothing is made to last anymore,
Lord. Products break down almost as soon as
I buy them. Expensive phones, computers, and
tablets go out of fashion before they're paid off.
Even relationships often come to a bitter end too
soon. But You, Lord? Your love will never fade,
no matter what I do. Your love has motivated
me to become a woman You can be proud of,
Father. I'm so grateful for that love. Amen.

OUR FATHER KNOWS BEST

Our Father in heaven always
knows what is best,
And if you trust in His wisdom,
your life will be blessed.

And we know that in all things God works for
the good of those who love him, who have
been called according to his purpose.
ROMANS 8:28 NIV

How are you comforted by the knowledge
that God has things under control?

Father, You know best. If there's a question to be
answered, I look to You. If I'm at a fork in the road,
I wait for Your voice. If I'm offered an opportunity
but don't know if I should take it, I rely on Your
guidance. You can see beyond today, well into all of
my tomorrows. So, I know I can trust Your wisdom
when You lead me from place to place, situation to
situation. Today I choose to trust You, Lord. Amen.

Day 114

THIS RESTLESS WORLD

Everyone has problems in
this restless world of care,
Everyone grows weary with
the cross they have to bear.

*And he said to all, "If any man would come
after me, let him deny himself and take
up his cross daily and follow me."*
LUKE 9:23

What crosses do you see friends and family
bearing? How can you help lighten the load?

---

*Sometimes it feels like too much, Lord. These
crosses I'm carrying are weighing me down.
The exhaustion I'm feeling has me doubting so
many things. But I trust You, Father. I also trust
You to help my friends and loved ones who seem
to be burdened down. You're the great Burden
Bearer, Lord. I pray that relief would come
swiftly to those who are hurting most. Amen.*

BATTLES WON

Thank God for good things
He has already done,
And be grateful to Him
For the battles you've won.

"For the battle is not yours, but God's."
2 CHRONICLES 20:15 NIV

What might God be creating
in your life right now?

---

*Sometimes I forget how far You've already brought
me, Lord. I look at the challenges ahead and lose all
recollection of the barricades You've already lifted
me over. I get scared, as if I've never had to depend
on You before. The truth is, You've never failed me,
Father, and I know You never will.
I can count on You. Amen.*

Day 116

RELIGHTED FAITH

When you're disillusioned,
And every hope is blighted,
Recall the promises of God,
And your faith will be relighted.

Never be lacking in zeal, but keep your spiritual
fervor, serving the Lord. Be joyful in hope,
patient in affliction, faithful in prayer.
ROMANS 12:11–12 NIV

Which of God's promises can you turn
to when you need encouragement?

Thank You for spiritual recall, Lord. I get
disillusioned at times and have a tendency to forget.
My hope seeps away. Then You remind me of Your
promises, Your provision, Your vast love for me,
and everything comes into alignment again. My
spiritual candle is relit. I'm so grateful, Lord. Amen.

Day 117

GOD'S PURPOSE

God never plows in the soul of man
Without intention and purpose and plan.

*It is the hard-working farmer who
ought to have the first share of the crops.*
2 TIMOTHY 2:6

What good has come out of
God's plowing in your life?

---

*Plowing can be painful, Lord. I see You digging
up weeds that have taken root in my heart
and wreaked havoc on the good fruit. I know
the plowing won't last forever. It's hard to say
"Thank You" during seasons such as this,
but that's exactly what I'm saying today,
Father. Thank You for plucking out the bad
and replacing it with the best. Amen.*

THE ANCHOR

God's love is like an anchor
When the angry billows roll—
A mooring in the storms of life,
A stronghold for the soul!

The LORD is my rock, and my fortress, and my deliverer,
my God, my rock, in whom I take refuge, my shield,
and the horn of my salvation, my stronghold.
PSALM 18:2

How do you find God in the storms of life?

I'm clinging tight to You today, Father. All
around me the storms are raging. If not for
my tight grasp on You, I would surely sink.
Thank You for being my fortress, my mooring,
my anchor. Even in the roughest seas I know I'm
safe. Praise You for holding me steady. Amen.

Day 119

SOMEBODY CARES

God forgives you until the end,
He is your faithful, loyal friend.
Somebody cares and loves you still,
And God is the Someone who always will.

*Bless the LORD, O my soul, and forget not all his
benefits, who forgives all your iniquity. . .who
crowns you with steadfast love and mercy,
who satisfies you with good as long as you live.*
PSALM 103:2–5

What characteristics do you look for in a friend?
What kind of friend are you?

---

*You're an "always" friend, Lord. When others
drift away, lose interest, bond to others, You will
stick close. You're quick to forgive my transgressions
and even quicker to sweep me into Your arms to
wash away my pain and fears. How grateful I
am for a friend like You, Father. Amen.*

BLESSINGS FROM ABOVE

Each day there are showers of blessings
Sent from the Father above,
For God is a great, lavish giver
And there is no end to His love.

Thou art the God who workest wonders,
who hast manifested thy might among the peoples.
PSALM 77:14

How can you be God's eyes today?

Teach me to be a lavish giver like You, Lord.
I want to be known as one who is generous to a
fault. May I learn from Your example, Father,
so that others can sense Your generosity every
time they are around me. May I shower love,
affection, and blessings on those in my
path today, Lord. Amen.

Day 121

DISGUISED BLESSINGS

God speaks to us in many ways,
Altering our lives, our plans and days,
And His blessings come in many guises
That He alone in love devises.

*"The LORD bless you and keep you: the LORD make his
face to shine upon you, and be gracious to you: the LORD
lift up his countenance upon you, and give you peace."*
NUMBERS 6:24–26

How do you communicate to your
family that you cherish them?

---

*I love the idea that You are "devising" blessings
to shower on me, Father! You're ready to surprise
me with something special. I can feel it. As You
speak into my life, I choose to listen so that I can,
in turn, bless others. Give me Your ideas, Your
surprises, Your vision for those I love. Amen.*

Day 122

JUST SMILE

You'll find when you smile,
Your day will be brighter
And all of your burdens
Will seem so much lighter.

I sought the LORD, and he answered me, and delivered me
from all my fears. Look to him, and be radiant.
PSALM 34:4–5

What makes you laugh?

Sometimes all it takes, Lord, is a smile from a
friend. A joyous expression lifts my soul and reminds
me that my problems, no matter how pressing, will
be gone tomorrow. In the meantime, I can choose joy.
Today, may I be a shining light, a smiling face,
to those I come in contact with. Amen.

Day 123

HOLY PLAN

"Take up your cross and follow Me,"
The Savior said to man,
"Trust always in the greatness
Of My Father's holy plan."

*God looks down from heaven upon the sons of men to see
if there are any that are wise, that seek after God.*
PSALM 53:2

Which aspect of God's character
means the most to you?

---

*Your plans are far superior to mine, Lord, and I'm
grateful. I know I can trust You to bring to fruition
all You have planned for my life. So even during the
"take up your cross" seasons, I choose to stay focused
on You, my Plan Giver. There is greatness ahead,
Father. I can sense it, even now. Praise You! Amen.*

Day 124

WHY?

Why am I impatient
And continually vexed
And often bewildered,
Disturbed and perplexed?

*Amazed and perplexed, they asked one
another, "What does this mean?"*
ACTS 2:12 NIV

What frustrates you about yourself?

---

*I'm impatient at times, Lord. I'll admit it.
And sometimes I let frustration guide me instead
of Your supernatural peace. Thank You for the
reminder that negative emotions should drive
me toward You, not away from You. You care
about my feelings, but You care enough to remind
me that You are greater than what I'm feeling.
I'm so grateful for that, Father. Amen.*

Day 125

STRENGTH FOR TODAY

God did not promise sun without rain,
Light without darkness
or joy without pain—
He only promised us strength for the day
When the darkness comes
and we lose our way.

You, LORD, keep my lamp burning;
my God turns my darkness into light.
PSALM 18:28 NIV

What positive things can come
from being in the dark?

I've walked some dark roads, Lord. There have
been times I didn't know which way to turn.
Confusion reigned. I'm so glad You have the
ability to counteract darkness with light, so that
my path can be illuminated. So many times You've
swept in to rescue me, turning sadness to joy,
fear to peace. I'm so grateful, Father. Amen.

Day 126

IN HIS HANDS

God only asks us to do our best,
Then He will take over and finish the rest.

But be doers of the word, and not hearers
only, deceiving yourselves.
JAMES 1:22

What is your spouse's or children's
most charming quality?

Father, I don't always give You my best.
Sometimes my efforts are halfhearted or apathetic.
Today I recommit myself to giving all of my efforts
to building a strong relationship with You and
with those You've placed in my life. I want to
be a doer, Lord. Help me, I pray. Amen.

Day 127

GOD HEARS

God hears every prayer
And He answers each one
When we pray in His name,
"Thy will be done."

*"I desire to do your will, my God;
your law is within my heart."*
PSALM 40:8 NIV

What service can you give the church this week?

---

*Sometimes it's hard to pray "Thy will be done,"
Lord, because (honestly) I'm usually more interested
in my own will being done. It's hard to submit
my will to Yours; but today I choose to do just that.
These things I'm hoping/wishing/dreaming for?
I place them at Your feet and say, "Your will, not
mine, Father." I know I can trust You. Amen.*

Day 128

HOLY SUNLIGHT

Flowers sleep beneath the ground,
But when they hear spring's waking sound,
They push themselves through layers of clay
To reach the sunlight of God's day.

"Truly, truly, I say to you, the hour is coming,
and now is, when the dead will hear the voice
of the Son of God, and those who hear will live."
JOHN 5:25

What is making your heart sing this morning?

I love those "happy heart" days, Father, when new
things are bursting forth in my soul, like flowers
pushing up from the dry earth. You bring all things
to life again, even the songs in my heart. Today I
offer You the hardened clay of my heart. Soften it,
I pray, that a "bursting forth" can take place. Amen.

Day 129

NATURE'S BEAUTY

Thank You, God, for the beauty
Around me everywhere,
The gentle rain and glistening dew,
The sunshine and the air.

The eyes of the LORD are in every place,
keeping watch on the evil and the good.
PROVERBS 15:3

Where do you see beauty?

My eyes are wide open, Father! I see beauty at every
turn—in a toddler's crooked grin, in a coworker's
sparkling eyes, in a blue sky, in a colorful rainbow,
in a mud puddle after the storm, in the morning
dew clinging to blades of grass. These things bring
joy to my soul and remind me that You care about
even the smallest details. You have surrounded me
with things of beauty! I'm so grateful, Lord. Amen.

Day 130

INFINITE BLESSINGS

God's grace is more than sufficient,
His mercy is boundless and deep,
And His infinite blessings are countless,
And all this we're given to keep.

*"Ask and it will be given to you; seek and you will find;
knock and the door will be opened to you."*
MATTHEW 7:7 NIV

In what ways have you counted
your blessings lately?

---

*I appreciate this reminder that I'm surrounded
by Your blessings, Lord. So many times I plow
forward, forgetting that these things I often take
for granted are Your gifts to me. Today I pause
and think through so many—my family, friends,
home, provision, and clothing. May I never
take Your gifts for granted, Father. Amen.*

Day 131

YOUR DEAREST WISH

Put your dearest wish in God's hands today
And discuss it with Him as you faithfully pray,
And you can be sure your wish will come true
If God feels that your wish will be good for you.

*Thy hands have made and fashioned me; give me
understanding that I may learn thy commandments.*
PSALM 119:73

How do you help fulfill dreams
of your family and friends?

---

*From the time I was a little girl, Lord, I've
been a dreamer. I always wanted every wish
to come true, every dream to come to fruition.
Today I place those dreams in Your capable
hands. I give them to You without reservation.
I humbly ask that You only bring the very best
ones to life, the ones that will fulfill me and
bring joy to Your heart. Thank You for caring
about my dreams, Lord. Amen.*

Day 132

HELP ME

Help me when I falter,
Hear me when I pray,
Receive me in Thy kingdom
To dwell with Thee someday.

*One thing have I asked of the LORD, that will I
seek after; that I may dwell in the house of the
LORD all the days of my life, to behold the beauty
of the LORD, and to inquire in his temple.*
PSALM 27:4

How have you overcome past fears?

---

*Father, I need Your continual help. I don't want
to forge ahead, doing things on my own. I cry out
to You today, Lord, because I know You care. You
hear every heart-cry and respond out of Your great
love. Even the deepest, darkest fears I place in
Your hands, because I know You will help me
overcome. I'm so grateful, Father. Amen.*

Day 133

FOREVER PROMISES

Know that the promises of God
Will never fail or falter,
And you will inherit everlasting life
Which even death cannot alter.

*Keep your life free from love of money,
and be content with what you have; for he has
said, "I will never fail you nor forsake you."*
HEBREWS 13:5

When have you fallen short
on a promise you've made?

---

*If You've said it, Lord, You will bring it to pass. I
never have to doubt Your promises. You've promised
me eternal life in heaven, and I can't wait to see
what that looks like. Until that day, mold me into
a promise keeper. Make me more like You so that I
can be a good witness to those I meet. Amen.*

A PRICELESS REWARD

Let me be great in the eyes of the Lord,
For that is the richest, most priceless reward.

The one who plants and the one who waters
have one purpose, and they will each be
rewarded according to their own labor.
1 CORINTHIANS 3:8 NIV

What are some acts for which
you'll be rewarded in heaven?

Lord, shift my thinking. I need to care more about
what You think about me than what others think.
Turn my people-pleasing eyes toward You, Father,
that I might live to make Your heart happy.
In doing so, those around me will see my heart,
my passion, for my Savior. I give myself to
You afresh today, Lord. Amen.

Day 135

HIS KIND BENEDICTION

When God sends sorrow
or some dread affliction,
Be assured that it comes
with His kind benediction.

*"I will turn their mourning into joy, I will
comfort them, and give them gladness for sorrow."*
JEREMIAH 31:13

Can you lend comfort to a friend this week?

---

*Sometimes life's sorrows seem too great, Lord.
I've suffered losses, pain, affliction. I've watched
those I love go through deep valleys. I'm so grateful
for the reminder that You will turn my sorrows
into joy. You will turn my mourning into dancing.
May my toes start tapping, even now. Turn
my eyes toward You, Father. Amen.*

Day 136

BE STILL

Let us plan with prayerful
care to always allocate
A certain portion of each
day to be still and meditate.

*"I will consider all your works and
meditate on all your mighty deeds."*
PSALM 77:12 NIV

What do you love best about Jesus?

---

*In Your presence, Lord, I find fullness of joy.
When I neglect to spend time with You,
my energy wanes, my joy fades, and challenges
seem harder than ever. In Your presence, all of
my cares are washed away as I'm overwhelmed
by Your great love and care. Today, I choose to
spend time with You, meditating on Your goodness.
What an amazing Father You are! Amen.*

Day 137

IN A FLOWER

Little do we realize
That the glory and the power
Of He who made the universe
Lies hidden in a flower.

*O LORD, our Lord, how majestic
is thy name in all the earth!*
PSALM 8:1

What does creation tell you about God's goodness?

---

*Your goodness surrounds me, Lord, even when
life's circumstances are hard. Nature provides
breathtaking reminders of Your glory, Your power,
Your desire to fill the earth with color and beauty.
Something as tiny as a butterfly serves as a vivid
reminder that You are in the details, Lord.
I love that about You! Amen.*

Day 138

HEART VISION

Love is unselfish, understanding, and kind,
For it sees with the heart and
not with the mind!

*He who does not love does not
know God; for God is love.*
1 JOHN 4:8

In what areas of your life do you need to use your
heart vision instead of your head vision?

_____

*Father, I'm so grateful for heart vision. There are
days when I only see the bad in people, but You're
reminding me that I need to have Your vision,
not my own. Your vision is gracious, grace filled,
empathetic, and kind. May I be more like You
as I see with Your eyes, Lord. Amen.*

BRIGHTEN YOUR CORNER

If everybody brightened up the
spot on which they're standing
By being more considerate
and a little less demanding,
This dark old world would very
soon eclipse the evening star—
If everybody brightened up
the corner where they are!

*"You, LORD, are my lamp; the LORD
turns my darkness into light."*
2 SAMUEL 22:29 NIV

What can be said about how you display
the fruit of the Spirit (Galatians 5:22–23)?

---

*Father, I long to brighten my corner of
the world. Help me lay aside my demands,
my wants, my wishes, to focus on others.
I want to be known as one who is considerate,
not one who is self-absorbed. Only You can
help me achieve that. When others look at me,
Lord, may they see You—in my actions,
my words, and my smile. Amen.*

Day 140

SILENT COMMUNION

Kneel in prayer in His presence,
And you'll find no need to speak,
For softly in silent communion,
God grants you the peace that you seek.

For God alone my soul waits in silence;
from him comes my salvation.
PSALM 62:1

Are you a peacemaker by nature?
How can you grow in this area?

I have to confess, Lord, that it's often hard
to maintain my silence. I want to be the one
telling You how to run things. But I'm learning,
Father, that the best way to make it through any
circumstance is to be still and know that You are
Lord. You don't need my help, my instructions,
my ideas. You, alone, know best. Today I choose
to listen. . .in silence. Speak clearly, Lord. Amen.

Day 141

ENDLESS LOVE

To know life is unending and
God's love is endless, too
Makes our daily tasks and burdens
so much easier to do.

For the wages of sin is death, but the free gift
of God is eternal life in Christ Jesus our Lord.
ROMANS 6:23

How have you been given mercy?

Lord, I love the word endless. *What an amazing*
word, and what a remarkable concept. Thanks to the
work Your Son did on the cross, this word is now a
lasting part of my vocabulary. I've been born again
to an endless life, one that will carry on after my
physical death into all eternity. It boggles my mind
and stirs my excitement, Father! And to think, the
journey has already begun! I'm so grateful. Amen.

Day 142

THE HAND OF GOD

In everything
Both great and small
We see the hand
Of God in all.

*Arise, O LORD; O God, lift up
thy hand; forget not the afflicted.*
PSALM 10:12

Where have you seen God this week?

---

*I feel like I'm always looking for You in the "big"
things, Father—miraculous healings, supernatural
provision, over-the-top stories that get me hyped
about serving You. But today I'm reminded that
even in the littlest of things, Your hand is still at
work in this world. May I never neglect to see You
right in front of me, in both big and small things.
What a wonder You are! Amen.*

Day 143

MEDITATION HOUR

Help us all to realize
There is untold strength and power
When we seek the Lord and find Him
In our meditation hour.

May all who seek thee rejoice and be glad in thee!
PSALM 70:4

How can you help a friend
strengthen her prayer life?

---

*I love the promise in Your Word, Lord, that if I seek
You, I will find You. Today I choose to do just that.
I ask that You use me to lead others into a deeper
commitment to You as well, Father. May all who
know me be drawn to the God they see in me.
Strengthen me during our together time that I
might be a great witness for You, Lord. Amen.*

Day 144

A RESTING PLACE

The road will grow much smoother
And much easier to face,
So do not be disheartened—
This is just a resting place.

My people will live in peaceful dwelling places,
in secure homes, in undisturbed places of rest.
ISAIAH 32:18 NIV

How has your patience been tested lately?

What a bumpy road I've traveled, Lord! Sometimes
my feet ached from all of the stones I've tripped over.
How I long for a smooth path. Oh, but the lessons
You've taught me during the rocky times? I wouldn't
trade those for anything. So, thank You for both
roads, Father—rocky and smooth. Amen.

EFFECTIVE SERVICE

Grant me faith and courage,
Put purpose in my days,
Show me how to serve Thee
In the most effective ways.

*Wait for the LORD; be strong, and let your
heart take courage; yea, wait for the LORD!*
PSALM 27:14

What ministry or service project
can you begin or renew?

---

*I want to be effective, Lord. No more coasting
along, content with the mundane. I want to do
great things for You, things that will make a
difference for eternity. This is going to take faith
and courage, but You're capable of giving me all
I need to step out with courage. Thank You for
propelling me forward, Father. Amen.*

Day 146

ENDURING LOVE

God's love endureth forever—
What a wonderful thing to know
When the tides of life run against you
And your spirit is downcast and low.

For great is his steadfast love toward
us; and the faithfulness of the LORD
endures for ever. Praise the LORD!
PSALM 117:2

How has the love of God or the
Church surprised you in the past?

Father, I'm so glad that old saying "All good
things must come to an end" isn't true! Your
vast love for me never ends. It started from the
moment I was created in my mother's womb and
will continue throughout eternity. No matter
what challenges I face, no matter how low I feel,
that love will embolden me to live above my
circumstances. Praise You! Amen.

Day 147

HAPPY DAYS

Spare me all trouble
And save me from sorrow—
May each happy day
Bring a brighter tomorrow.

*"Look at the birds of the air: they neither sow nor reap
nor gather into barns, and yet your heavenly Father
feeds them. Are you not of more value than they?"*
MATTHEW 6:26

How has God's love and care
brought you reassurance?

_____

*Father, I would love to say that I had been spared
every pain, every heartache. But I know that's not
really how things work. Instead, I'm happy to say
that You have walked with me through every valley
and have given me the promise of better days ahead.
Thank You for that reassurance today, Lord. Amen.*

Day 148

HIGHER GROUND

In this world of trouble,
with darkness all around,
Take my hand and lead me until
I stand on higher ground.

*When Jesus spoke again to the people, he said, "I am
the light of the world. Whoever follows me will never
walk in darkness, but will have the light of life."*
JOHN 8:12 NIV

How do you feel when you help others?
Who needs your help today?

---

*I feel so safe, knowing Your hand is in mine,
Lord. I'll follow wherever You lead as long as You
never let go. You lead me from mountain peak to
mountain peak, carefully navigating the low areas
in between. I'm so grateful for the safety of Your
hand, Father. Thank You so much. Amen.*

OPPOSITES

Life is a mixture of sunshine and rain,
Laughter and teardrops, pleasure and pain,
Low tides and high tides, mountains and plains,
Triumphs, defeats and losses and gains.

For every matter has its time and way,
although man's trouble lies heavy upon him.
ECCLESIASTES 8:6

Reflect on your own life. In what areas can
you pinpoint the highs and lows? What
have you learned from them?

Lord, some would argue that the Christian walk
is blissful and easy. I would say the opposite!
My journey has been filled with high highs and
low lows. Sometimes I arrive on a mountaintop,
only to plummet back down to the valley without
warning. No matter what I'm facing, Father,
I know I can trust You to hold tight to my hand
all the way. Thank You, Lord. Amen.

Day 150

THIS IS ME

Each time you pick a daffodil
Or gather violets on some hill
Or touch a leaf or see a tree,
It's all God whispering, "This is Me."

*Seek the LORD and his strength, seek his presence
continually! Remember the wonderful works that he has
done, his miracles, and the judgments he uttered.*
PSALM 105:4–5

How can you use your creativity for God's glory?

---

*I will never understand how people can walk
through this life, oblivious to Your presence,
Lord. It's all around us! Do they not see the
blossoms on the trees, the golden rays of a sunset,
the majestic waves of the ocean? Oh, Father,
speak to those who claim You don't exist.
Draw them with Your creation, Lord, that
they might come to know You as I do. Amen.*

Day 151

FOREVER TRUE

When God makes a promise,
It remains forever true,
For everything God promises,
He unalterably will do.

And this is what he promised us—eternal life.
1 JOHN 2:25 NIV

What promises has God kept in your life?
What promises does He continue to keep?

---

*I'm surrounded by people who fall down on
the job, Lord. Their intentions are good, but they
don't always follow through. My ability to trust
them is waning. That's why I appreciate Your
Word, Father. I never have to wonder if You really
mean it when You whisper something into my
ear. What a trustworthy God You are! Amen.*

LIFE'S LADDER

As you climb life's ladder,
Take faith along with you,
And great will be your happiness
As your dearest dreams come true.

Love the LORD, all you his saints! The LORD
preserves the faithful, but abundantly
requites him who acts haughtily.
PSALM 31:23

When in your life do you feel your faith is
the strongest? The weakest? What have
you learned from these times?

My faith has been challenged so many times,
Lord. I climb the rungs of life's ladder, eyes focused
heavenward, then stumble and fall, my gaze
shifting downward as I temporarily lose my way.
Keep my faith strong, I pray, no matter how
difficult the climb, Father. May I never
doubt Your goodness, Lord. Amen.

Day 153

I STILL BELIEVE

Although I cannot find Your hand
To lead me on to the promised land,
I still believe with all my being
Your hand is there beyond my seeing!

"I, the LORD, have called you in righteousness;
I will take hold of your hand."
ISAIAH 42:6 NIV

How can you cultivate an atmosphere
of faith in your home?

There are times when my faith wanes, Lord. . .
when I can't seem to see past my circumstances to
Your hand. Help me to see, even when things don't
make sense—to trust that You're still right there,
hand extended, ready to lead me forward. With
all my being, Lord, I open my heart to trusting
Your will, Your plan for my life. Amen.

Day 154

HE NEVER CHANGES

I am perplexed and often vexed,
And sometimes I cry and sadly sigh,
But do not think, dear Father above,
I question You or Your unchanging love.

Have mercy on me, O God, according to your
unfailing love; according to your great
compassion blot out my transgressions.
PSALM 51:1 NIV

How do you outwardly show
that you are devoted to God?

You know my heart, Lord. It is often riddled
with confusion and concern. I do my best to keep
a stiff upper lip, but sometimes I slip up. During
these rough seasons, Father, please have mercy
on me. Increase my faith. Your love for me is
unchanging, no matter what sort of turmoil I'm
feeling in this fickle heart of mine. May I
never forget Your great love. Amen.

Day 155

TRUE FRIENDS

When you ask God for a gift,
Be thankful if He sends
Not diamonds, pearls, or riches,
But the love of real, true friends.

A good name is to be chosen rather than great riches,
and favor is better than silver or gold.
PROVERBS 22:1

How can you show your friends your
thankfulness for their place in your life?

I've asked for so many things from You, Lord—
provision, health, and more. And You've answered
my prayers in such an overwhelming way. Each
answer is a gift in itself. May I never forget that one
of the most precious gifts You've ever given me is the
gift of friendship. Greater than any possession is the
love of a good friend. I'm so grateful, Father. Amen.

Day 156

LET HIM IN

Open your heart's door
and let Christ come in,
And He will give you new life
and free you from sin,
And there is no joy that can ever compare
With the joy of knowing
you're in God's care.

*"I am the door; if any one enters by me, he will be saved,
and will go in and out and find pasture."*
JOHN 10:9

How can you spread the joy of
Christ to others this week?

---

*Lord, I open the door of my heart today. I swing it
wide. Step inside, Father. Be welcome in this place.
Do the work that You long to do, sweeping out the
cobwebs and clearing away any debris that comes
between us. I give myself to You afresh today, Lord.
My heart is Yours. Do with it as You will. Amen.*

Day 157

No Night

I am faith and I am light,
And in Me there shall be no night.

God is light; in him there is no darkness at all.
1 John 1:5 niv

How can you make a difference
with a passionate heart for Christ?

---

*No darkness at all. How amazing are those
words, Lord. With You all things are visible.
There are no deep, dark secrets. You have no secret
agendas, no twisted motivations. Only love.
Only light. And because You're the great Illuminator,
I can trust You with the road ahead. My faith
is strong, Lord. My heart is passionate. I'm so
grateful You light my way. Amen.*

Day 158

ADD SUNSHINE

To live a little better,
Always be forgiving.
Add a little sunshine
To the world in which we're living.

If your enemy is hungry, give him bread to eat;
and if he is thirsty, give him water to drink.
PROVERBS 25:21

How can you shine a light outside
your comfort zone today?

I want to be known as someone who spreads
sunshine wherever I go, Lord. No doom and
gloom from these lips! May I always be a
reflection of faith, hope, and perseverance.
This world needs hope, and I want to be the
first in line to offer it, Father. Thanks for
using me to do just that. Praise You! Amen.

GRANT ME...

God, grant me courage
and hope for every day,
Faith to guide me along my way,
Understanding and wisdom, too,
And grace to accept what life gives me to do.

Be strong, and let your heart take courage,
all you who wait for the LORD!
PSALM 31:24

When have you had to be courageous?

Sometimes I feel like the cowardly lion, Lord. I
square my shoulders and try to look brave, but on
the inside I'm quivering in fear. Thank You for the
reminder that courage is something You grant.
It comes from Your hand. I don't have to summon
it up or pretend to be brave. You can give me all
the courage I need when I most need it. I can be
strong in You. Thank You, Father! Amen.

Day 160

NEAR TO HIM

There is happiness in knowing
That my heart will always be
A place where I can hold You
And keep You near to me.

*Honor the LORD with your substance and
with the first fruits of all your produce.*
PROVERBS 3:9

What is God saying to you today?

---

*May I always have a heart that honors
You, God. I want my loyalty to You to drive
every move I make in every area of my life—
relationships, job, talents, abilities, and so on.
May I produce the fruits of a loyal daughter in
good seasons and bad. No wavering in this heart,
Lord! Thank You for keeping me close. Amen.*

Day 161

WONDROUS WISDOM

God has many messengers
We fail to recognize,
But He sends them when we need them,
For His ways are wondrous wise!

Do not neglect to show hospitality to strangers,
for thereby some have entertained angels unawares.
HEBREWS 13:2

How have you shown someone a kindness
and become an unexpected blessing?

I love how You speak to me through others I
meet along life's journey, Lord. At just the right
moment You send someone to say the very words
I need to hear. May I never forget that You care
enough to place just the right people in my life,
speaking messages of hope, encouragement, and
joy. May I be that kind of friend for others
as well. Thank You, Lord. Amen.

Day 162

LISTEN

Teach me to let go, dear God,
And pray undisturbed until
My heart is filled with inner peace
And I learn to know Your will!

*Every way of a man is right in his own eyes,
but the LORD weighs the heart.*
PROVERBS 21:2

How have you previously known
you were in God's will?

---

*Letting go isn't easy, Father. My fingers want to
tightly grip the things—and people—I love. But
You're teaching me that, in letting go of good things,
I can have the best. What peace floods my soul as I
realize You have my best interest at heart! May I
trust You as You tell me when to release my grip,
Lord. Give me courage, I pray. Amen.*

Day 163

DIVINE ASSISTANCE

Our future will seem brighter and
we'll meet with less resistance
If we call upon our Father and
seek divine assistance.

*Surely there is a future,
and your hope will not be cut off.*
PROVERBS 23:18

How can you provide hope to others?

---

*I don't always like to ask for help, Lord.
I'm one of those do-it-yourselfers. But You're
teaching me that asking for help isn't a sign of
weakness; it's a sign of strength. May I never
forget that You've got a terrific future planned
for me, one filled with surprises. This brings
me great hope, Lord! Thank You! Amen.*

Day 164

IT TAKES A MIXTURE

With nothing but sameness
how dull life would be,
For only life's challenge
can set the soul free,
And it takes a mixture of
both bitter and sweet
To season our lives and
make them complete.

"Blessed be the name of God for ever and ever,
to whom belong wisdom and might.
He changes times and seasons."
DANIEL 2:20–21

How can you encourage someone today?

I'm not a fan of bitter moments, Lord. In fact,
I would prefer to avoid them altogether. But I do
understand the concept: the sweet moments are all
the sweeter if I've been through the not-so-sweet
ones. Today I submit myself to the "mixture" of bitter
and sweet, Father. Help me to appreciate both;
for together, they make my life complete. Amen.

UNEXPECTED WAYS

God, make us conscious
That Your love comes in many ways,
And not always just as happiness
And bright and shining days.

*I will come and proclaim your mighty acts, Sovereign
Lord; I will proclaim your righteous deeds, yours alone.*
PSALM 71:16 NIV

How did God's love on a really
tough day make a difference?

---

*Walking with You is an adventure, Lord.
I've come to expect the unexpected. You surprise
me in so many ways and always keep me on my
toes. I'm grateful for those surprises, Father. What
a blessing they are, both on good days and bad.
I can't wait to see what You have in store for me
next, Father. I sense adventures ahead! Amen.*

TREASURED FRIENDS

Often during a busy day,
Pause for a minute and silently pray,
Mention the names of those you love
And treasured friends you're fondest of.

*The LORD has heard my supplication;
the LORD accepts my prayer.*
PSALM 6:9

How does prayer abate your worries?

---

*Worries arise at every turn, Father, and I often
forget that I could stop—right then and there—
and cry out to You. I call a friend, send an email
or text, or mope around. . .when I should be turning
to You for advice and comfort. Thank You
for the reminder that You are always nearby,
ready to hear my concerns. I'm grateful for
Your steady presence, Lord. Amen.*

Day 167

FRAGRANCE

You can't pluck a rose
all fragrant with dew
Without part of its fragrance
remaining with you.

Cast your bread upon the waters,
for you will find it after many days.
ECCLESIASTES 11:1

How can you influence your world today?

Father, I love the idea that I carry a heavenly
fragrance because of my relationship with You.
When people bump up against me, Lord, may
they only sense You and nothing more. I want to
be a good witness to all I come in contact with.
May Your heavenly fragrance linger long after
I've parted ways with them, I pray. Amen.

He Holds It All

Somehow the good Lord gives
us the power to understand
That He who holds tomorrow
is the One who holds our hand.

*If I take the wings of the morning and dwell in
the uttermost parts of the sea, even there thy hand
shall lead me, and thy right hand shall hold me.*
Psalm 139:9–10

How well do you rely on God and
trust Him to guide your way?

*You hold it all, Lord. Every created thing is
held into place by Your capable hand. You don't
just hold "things," Father; You hold our days too.
You held our yesterdays. Our tomorrows are tight
in Your grasp, and today is in Your palm. Knowing
I'm held by You brings me such peace. I know I
can trust You, Father. I'm so grateful. Amen.*

Day 169

LOVE IS A JOURNEY

Love is a journey through the years,
With peaks of joy and vales of tears—
A journey two folks take together
Hand-in-hand through wind and weather.

"For this reason a man shall leave his father
and mother and be joined to his wife,
and the two shall become one."
EPHESIANS 5:31

How can you keep love alive with your spouse
through the ups and downs of life?

I love the analogy of relationships being like a
journey, Lord. It's so true. Sometimes the road
is easy; other times it's a rugged terrain. In
good times and bad I'm grateful for the many
relationships You've brought into my life over
the years (whether romantic or friendship).
I've learned so much, Father. May each
relationship grow stronger with time. Amen.

Day 170

KINDNESS

Like roses in a garden,
Kindness fills the air
With a certain bit of sweetness
As it touches everywhere.

A gentle tongue is a tree of life,
but perverseness in it breaks the spirit.
PROVERBS 15:4

Do you struggle with taming your tongue?
Have you asked for help yet?

People can be so brusque to one another, Lord.
They buzz by, bumping shoulders, all in a rush
to get to that next place. Thank You for the
reminder that kindness is key. All it takes is a
warm smile to lift someone's spirits. A kind word
goes a long way in bringing encouragement.
Today, may I be Your hand extended as I offer
kindness to those around me. Amen.

Day 171

Timelessness

There is nothing that is new
beneath God's timeless sun,
And present, past, and future
are all molded into one.

*What has been will be again, what has been done will
be done again; there is nothing new under the sun.*
ECCLESIASTES 1:9 NIV

When have you felt God's unconditional love?

*You are timeless, Lord. You never change. You
are the same yesterday, today, and forever. I'm
so grateful for Your consistency. If You performed
miracles yesterday, You are still capable of
performing them today. I have nothing to fear,
Father, because You remain ever faithful,
ever true. Thank You. Amen.*

Day 172

WHEN HE COMES

The restless, unknown longing
of my searching soul won't cease
Until God comes in glory and
my soul at last finds peace.

*"Peace I leave with you; my peace I give to you;
not as the world gives do I give to you. Let not
your hearts be troubled, neither let them be afraid."*
JOHN 14:27

How do you get away to relax and rejuvenate?

---

*I live for Your return, Lord. One day—in the
blink of an eye—all of my troubles, my concerns,
my woes, will fade away. On that day, I'll
step into my happily-ever-after with You. My
restlessness, my longings, my frustrations will cease.
From that day on, I will only know Your vast,
unimaginable peace. I can't wait, Father! Amen.*

Day 173

A HIGHWAY

Life is a highway on which the years go by—
Sometimes the road is level,
sometimes the hills are high.

I lift up my eyes to the mountains—where does
my help come from? My help comes from the
LORD, the Maker of heaven and earth.
PSALM 121:1–2 NIV

What have you learned from the choices
you've made this week—good or bad?

What a fascinating road this is, Lord. There
are days when I trudge along, convinced I'll
never make it over the next hill. Then there
are other days when I coast along, not a care in
the world. When I look back over my journey,
I realize that I'm just as grateful for the hard
times as the good. I've learned so much,
Father, on this magnificent road. Amen.

Day 174

WHO BUT GOD?

Who can see the dawn break through
Without a glimpse of heaven and You?
For who but God could make the day
And softly put the night away?

*For salvation is nearer to us now than when we first
believed; the night is far gone, the day is at hand.*
ROMANS 13:11–12

What do you like about the dark? Do you
find it easier to be still and know that
He is God in the dark or in the light?

---

*Father, I love living in the light.
No stumble-bumbling for me, as long as Your
radiance leads the way. The early morning hours
take my breath away as I watch You "put the
night away" so that the sunlight can burst through.
Most of all, I'm grateful that You're with me, even
when the night skies rock me to sleep. You're an
ever-present Father, and I'm so grateful. Amen.*

Day 175

ANGELS ALL AROUND

Keep looking for an angel
And keep listening to hear,
For on life's busy, crowded streets
You will find God's presence near.

"Thou hast made known to me the ways of life;
thou wilt make me full of gladness with thy presence."
ACTS 2:28

What has been your greatest blessing today?

You're as close as my next heartbeat, Lord.
Ever present. Always right there, ready to
sweep in and rescue, deliver, save. . . I will
keep my ear inclined to You so I can hear Your
voice, no matter how crowded or busy my life
might get. Your brings me such joy! Amen.

Day 176

OUR FUTURE

God, renew our spirits and
make us more aware
That our future is dependent
on sacrifice and prayer.

*"And all these blessings shall come upon you and overtake
you, if you obey the voice of the LORD your God."*
DEUTERONOMY 28:2

What are some of your favorite hymns?
What effect do these songs have on you?

---

*Today I ask for a renewal, Lord—of my heart, my
thoughts, and my physical body. From this day forth,
may I be more aware of the role You play in my life.
May I never forget that You've called me to a life of
service and prayer. My antenna is up, Father. I lean
in Your direction, ready to do Your will. Amen.*

ONE PLACE TO GO

There's but one place to go,
and that is to God,
And, dropping all pretense and pride,
We can pour out our problems
without restraint
And gain strength with
the Lord at our side.

For I, the LORD your God, hold your right hand;
it is I who say to you, "Fear not, I will help you."
ISAIAH 41:13

Where is your best "prayer closet"
to get one-on-one with God?

You know me better than anyone, Lord—
my motives, my thoughts, my ambitions.
When will I learn that You are the One who
cares the most? Today I choose to run straight
into Your arms, bypassing all others. It's
Your truth that matters most to me, Father.
So, I let go of pride, of pretense, and rush to
be with You and no one else. What an
amazing Father You are! Amen.

Day 178

TAKE MY HAND

Father, I am well aware
I can't make it on my own,
So take my hand and hold it tight,
For I cannot walk alone.

*Though I walk in the midst of trouble, thou dost preserve
my life; thou dost stretch out thy hand against the wrath
of my enemies, and thy right hand delivers me.*
PSALM 138:7

Do you know someone who needs
a shoulder to lean on right now?

---

*There have been so many times that I've reached
out my hand, hoping for someone—something—
to steady me. Lord, You are the only One who can
hold me upright when everything around me is
slipping and sliding. The path is treacherous at
times, and I won't make it on my own. I'm so
grateful You've extended Your helping hand
in my direction, Father. Amen.*

GOD'S WHISPERS

Each time you look up in the sky
Or watch the fluffy clouds drift by
Or touch a leaf or see a tree,
It's all God whispering, "This is Me."

The heavens are telling the glory of God;
and the firmament proclaims his handiwork.
PSALM 19:1

How is gentleness exemplified in the women
around you? How do you show gentleness?

Your gentle hand is at work all around me, Father.
I glance up at wispy white clouds and sense Your
presence. I gaze at a clear blue sky and marvel at
Your color choices. Even the very ground I walk
on is evidence of Your creative hand at work.
You hold all things together, Lord. And with
every move I make, I am made more aware
of Your goodness toward us. Amen.

Day 180

PEACE, BE STILL

I know He stilled the tempest
and calmed the angry sea,
And I humbly ask if in His love
He'll do the same for me.

*And he awoke and rebuked the wind,
and said to the sea, "Peace! Be still!" And the
wind ceased, and there was a great calm.*
MARK 4:39

Do you desire more peace in your life?
How can you better manage your
schedule to provide some downtime?

---

*Life is churning all around me, Lord. It seems
like everyone's in turmoil, riddled with anxiety,
rushing to get from here to there. In the middle
of it all, Father, I yearn for peace. I want to lay
down my angst and draw a deep breath. Today
I ask You to rebuke the storms inside my heart,
Father. Whisper, "Peace, be still!" that my heart
might rest, calm and comfortable in Your
embrace. I love You, Lord. Amen.*

LET GO AND LET GOD

Rest and relax and grow stronger,
Let go and let God share your load,
Your work is not finished or ended,
You've just come to a bend in the road.

Trust in the LORD *with all your heart, and do not
rely on your own insight. In all your ways acknowledge
him, and he will make straight your paths.*
PROVERBS 3:5–6

What is causing stress in your life? How often
do you feel overloaded and overwhelmed?

*I've heard the expression all my life, Lord:
Let go and let God. It's easy to say, but not as
easy to do. Relinquishing my hold on things is
tougher than I imagined, but today I choose to
do just that. Help me release my stranglehold on
situations, Father. I truly long to be released so
that You can do Your perfect work while I submit
to Your will. I need Your help, Lord! Amen.*

Day 182

A Quiet Peace

Where there is love there is a smile
To make all things seem more worthwhile,
Where there is love there's a quiet peace,
A tranquil place where turmoils cease.

So faith, hope, love abide, these three;
but the greatest of these is love.
1 Corinthians 13:13

What activity (in which you're normally not
interested) can you share with your family
that will show them your love?

There aren't a lot of tranquil moments in my life,
Lord. As You know, I'm on the go much of the time.
Seems like chaos reigns most days. I long for the kind
of peace only You can offer. Show me Your kind of
tranquility, Father, that I might share it with those
I love. Thank You for abundant peace, Lord. Amen.

Day 183

UNEXPECTED MIRACLES

The unexpected kindness
from an unexpected place,
A hand outstretched in friendship,
a smile on someone's face,
A word of understanding
spoken in a time of trial
Are unexpected miracles that
make life more worthwhile.

Share with the Lord's people who are in need.
ROMANS 12:13 NIV

What is something unexpected you could do today?

---

*Your timing is perfect, Lord. You send people
with an encouraging word, a handshake, a greeting
. . .at just the right moment. Warm smiles give me
courage to keep going when I'm convinced I cannot.
Friendly words offer hope when I'm feeling down
in the dumps. In short, Your people bring me
hope, Father. Thank You! Amen.*

Day 184

GOD'S OPEN HANDS

When trouble surrounds you
And no one understands,
Try placing your cares
In God's open hands.

Thou hatest those who pay regard to
vain idols; but I trust in the LORD.
PSALM 31:6

Do you struggle with pessimism? What are
five things you can look forward to today?

Your hands are wide open, Lord! I love that image.
You don't shut me out or close me off from Your
presence. You make Yourself available to me, no
matter what I've done or how far I've stepped
away from You. Thank You for approaching Your
kids with open hands, Father. How good and
generous You are to all of us. I'm so thankful! Amen.

His Love Is Near

The earth is where we live today,
And we must serve God here,
For He watches us from way up there,
And His love is always near.

*"But whoever would be great among you must be
your servant, and whoever would be first among
you must be your slave; even as the Son of man
came not to be served but to serve, and to give
his life as a ransom for many."*
Matthew 20:26–28

As you admire the night sky, what do the
heavens, with its stars, galaxies, and
planets, tell you about God?

---

*Lord, I can only imagine what heaven will
be like. From here on earth, I do my best to
picture it all, but it's beyond my comprehension.
You're such a creative God. The earth is filled
with vibrant colors, magnificent wonders. . .all
straight from Your hand. I'm sure it's all just a
foretaste of what's to come in heaven, Lord.
What a marvelous day it will be when I see it
all for the firsttime. I can't wait, Lord. Amen!*

Day 186

Endless Hope

I come to meet You, God, and as I linger here,
I seem to feel You very near—
A rustling leaf, a rolling slope
Speak to my heart of endless hope.

*"From the fig tree learn its lesson: as soon as its branch
becomes tender and puts forth its leaves, you know that
summer is near. So also, when you see these things taking
place, you know that he is near, at the very gates."*
MARK 13:28–29

Are you awaiting Christ's ever-near return
with hope? What will it be like to
speak with Him face-to-face?

---

*Where would I be without my hope, Lord?
I would have given up years ago. But You
keep restoring it, even when all seems lost.
Nature itself gives me reasons to keep going.
So I continue to wait with great expectation,
Father. I refuse to let go. I won't give up.
In fact, my anticipation is building, even now.
I praise You for this hope, Lord. Amen.*

GROWTH IN TROUBLES

There's a lot of comfort in the thought
That sorrow, grief, and woe
Are sent into our lives sometimes
To help our souls to grow.

In the fear of the LORD one has strong confidence,
and his children will have a refuge.
PROVERBS 14:26

Where is your place of refuge? How have you
seen growth in your life during times of trial?

If troubles cause my soul to grow, Lord, then I'm
growing daily! It feels like I'm surrounded by
troubles on every side. Still, I'm comforted by the
thought that You're right here, growing me into a
woman You can be proud of. No matter what I go
through, Father, no matter what difficulties I face,
I choose to keep my focus on You so I can learn
from even the toughest experiences. Amen.

Day 188

A REASON TO REJOICE

In trouble and in gladness
We can always hear Your voice
If we listen in the silence
And find a reason to rejoice.

"Then you shall call, and the LORD will answer;
you shall cry, and he will say, Here I am."
ISAIAH 58:9

How can you praise God for what you see today?

I'm not a very good listener, Lord. My mouth
is usually open—giving advice, rambling on,
chattering about anything and everything. Today
I choose to sit in silence and listen for Your still,
small voice. Even during troubled times, You're
speaking—if I can remain silent long enough to
hear what You're saying. I'm leaning in close today,
Father. Speak to my heart, I pray. Amen.

DAILY BLESSINGS

We rob our own lives much
more than we know
When we fail to respond or in any way show
Our thanks for the blessings
that are daily ours—
The warmth of the sun,
the fragrance of flowers.

All thy works shall give thanks to thee, O LORD,
and all thy saints shall bless thee! They shall speak
of the glory of thy kingdom, and tell of thy power,
to make known to the sons of men thy mighty deeds,
and the glorious splendor of thy kingdom.
PSALM 145:10–12

How can you recognize today
what you usually take for granted?

How often I forget to thank You for daily
blessings, Father! They surround me on every
side, and yet I often take them for granted. Today
I ask You to forgive me for overlooking Your vast
goodness. May I remain in awe, day in and day
out, as I witness firsthand Your many miracles.
All of creation gives thanks to You, Lord. May
I never forget to praise You for this. Amen.

Day 190

Teach Me

Lord, show me the way
I can somehow repay
The blessings You've given to me. . .
Lord, teach me to do what
You most want me to
And to be what You want me to be.

What shall I return to the LORD for all his goodness
to me? . . . I will fulfill my vows to the LORD.
PSALM 116:12, 14 NIV

How do you feel about your role as wife, mother,
daughter, caregiver, and so on? What do you
struggle with? What do you enjoy?

Sometimes I overlook the abundant blessings You've
bestowed on me, Lord. I forget that every good and
perfect gift is just that. . .a gift. I want to show my
thanks by spreading Your love, Your mercy, and
Your grace to all I come in contact with. May they
experience Your goodness through my actions, Father.
I want to be a great witness for You. Amen.

Day 191

HE IS AWARE

Our Father up in heaven
Is very much aware
Of our failures and shortcomings
And the burdens that we bear.

*My flesh and my heart may fail, but God is the
strength of my heart and my portion for ever.*
PSALM 73:26

How aware of God are you in your day-to-day duties?
How can you become more aware of Him?

*I'll admit it, Lord: sometimes I rehearse my
shortcomings. I play them over in my head and
convince myself that things will never change.
Give me Your perspective, Father. I want to go
easier on myself so that I don't end up frozen
in place. Yes, I'm flawed, but You are teaching
me how to keep moving forward in spite of
my shortcomings. I love You, Lord.*

Day 192

TRUE PERFECTION

Wonder of wonders,
beyond man's conception,
For only in God can love
find true perfection.

The LORD is gracious and compassionate,
slow to anger and rich in love.
PSALM 145:8 NIV

Do you have a temper? How does
anger affect those around you?

I love imperfectly, Lord. I try so hard, but my
patience with people often wears thin. I snap.
I say things I shouldn't. Today I ask for Your kind of
love, Father. May I be long on patience and short on
anger. May my heart extend to those with differences
of opinion, not just those who agree with me.
In other words, Father, may I love like You love. Amen.

HE GIVES ME STRENGTH

If God does not ease my load,
He will give me strength to bear it,
For God in love and mercy
is always near to share it.

*When you are in distress and all these things have
happened to you, then in later days you will return to the
LORD your God and obey him. For the LORD your God is
a merciful God; he will not abandon or destroy you.*
DEUTERONOMY 4:30–31 NIV

Are you a leader or a follower?
How are you at teamwork?

Distress. *It's not a word I enjoy, Lord. I seem
to have a lot of it in my life. I know that You're
the Burden Bearer, but sometimes I feel like I'm
carrying a lot of weight. Today, I place my burdens,
my fears, my concerns into Your capable hands.
What I cannot do on my own, Father, I give to You.
You will never abandon me, even in my hour
of distress. My heart is thankful. Amen.*

Day 194

I HAVE YOU

My blessings are so many,
my troubles are so few,
How can I feel discouraged
when I know that I have You?

*"Be strong and courageous. Do not be afraid;
do not be discouraged, for the LORD your
God will be with you wherever you go."*
JOSHUA 1:9 NIV

How can you be God's voice today? Who do you
know that needs to be encouraged by His truth?

---

*Lord, if I put my blessings on the scale, they would
far outweigh the woes. Help me to remember that.
May I never forget that Your mighty hand is at
work, even during the toughest times, and that You
can turn a test into a testimony. In the meantime,
give me courage to keep moving forward. I want to
pass this test, Lord! Help me, I pray. Amen.*

Day 195

HERE COMES THE SUN

Have patience to wait for the day
When the sun comes out
and the clouds float away!

*The Mighty One, God the LORD, speaks and summons
the earth from the rising of the sun to its setting.*
PSALM 50:1

How can you make the world
around you a better place today?

---

*Sometimes I feel like daylight will never come,
Lord. . .that I'm stuck in the dark, difficult seasons
forever. Thank You for the reminder that morning
will dawn. The sun will burst through in all its
splendor, casting away night's shadows and bringing
hope along with it. While I'm waiting, Father,
give me patience. I want to be found with a smile
on my face when those clouds float away. Amen.*

Day 196

RICH BLESSINGS

May He who sends the raindrops
And makes the sunshine, too,
Look down and bless you richly
And be very near to you!

Thou hast fixed all the bounds of the earth;
thou hast made summer and winter.
PSALM 74:17

How can you cultivate an atmosphere
of thankfulness in your home?

You send it all, Father—the sunshine and the rain.
Every season, easy or tough, is under Your control.
I know You can be trusted, Lord. You're close by.
So, today I choose to thank You, even though
everything in my life isn't perfect. (Far from it,
in fact.) I thank You because You're growing me
into a mighty woman of God, one with deep
roots. Praise You, Father. Amen.

SWEET SURPRISE

Make us more aware, dear God,
Of little daily graces
That come to us with sweet surprise
From never-dreamed-of places.

O my God, in thee I trust.
PSALM 25:2

What one word best describes
God to you today? Why?

---

*I love Your surprises, Lord! Oh, those little blessings
that come from unexpected places—how they bring
me joy! May I never neglect to see Your hand at
work in each tiny thing, for You are always ready
to delight me. May I be found grateful, Father,
and ready to bless those around me just as You are
blessing me. Help me spread Your love, I pray. Amen.*

LITTLE THINGS

Little prayers for little things
Fly heavenward on little wings,
And no prayer is too great or small
To ask of God who hears them all.

Keep me as the apple of the eye;
hide me in the shadow of thy wings.
PSALM 17:8

What "little things" do you typically
not take to God in prayer?

You're a God of details! Sometimes I forget, Lord.
I don't take the trivial things to You in prayer
because I don't want to bother You. But You're never
bothered by my concerns, my requests. There's nothing
too big or small for You. I'm the apple of Your eye,
and You care about it all equally, Father. From now
on, I'll bring it all to Your throne, Lord, because I
know You care about the small things too. Amen.

Day 199

THE PEACEFUL HARBOR

God's love is like a harbor
Where our souls can find sweet rest
From the struggle and the tension
Of life's fast and futile quest.

They were glad when it grew calm,
and he guided them to their desired haven.
PSALM 107:30 NIV

What Bible verse helps you to imagine
God being your harbor of rest?

You're my harbor, Lord. I can rest in that safe, quiet
place, waters gently rocking me back and forth.
When I find myself overwhelmed, I will choose to
pull into peaceful waters for a season of rest and
reflection. You long for me to spend time with You,
away from the chaos of this world. Today I pull near,
ready to hear Your voice. As I do, tension fades away,
Lord. I'm so thankful for Your peace. Amen.

Day 200

THERE MUST BE RAIN

Our Father knows what's best for us,
So why should we complain?
We always want the sunshine,
But He knows there must be rain.

Do everything without grumbling or arguing.
PHILIPPIANS 2:14 NIV

What seemingly insurmountable task
can you ask God to help you with?

---

*I don't want to be a complainer, Lord. Please
shift my focus today off the trivial annoyances
and onto Your goodness. May I spend less time
focusing on the rain and more time focusing on
the sunshine. There's plenty of it in my life, Father!
Even when tasks seem too great, even when
challenges feel too overwhelming, I'm grateful for
the reminder that they are growing me into a
strong and mighty woman of God. Amen.*

Day 201

HE'S THE TREE

We, too, must be dependent
on our Father up above,
For we are but the branches,
and He's the tree of love.

"Blessed are those who wash their robes,
that they may have the right to the tree of life
and may go through the gates into the city."
REVELATION 22:14 NIV

Imagine yourself in a peaceful, quiet place.
What is God whispering to you in the wind?

I long to be a beautiful extension of You, Lord.
May my roots be planted deep in Your Word,
Your plan, Your love. Without You, I would be
nothing, Father. Absolutely nothing. But,
working in tandem with You, I'm capable of
great things. Use me to reach this world, I pray,
as I remain rooted in You, Lord. Amen.

Day 202

MORNING MEETING

The sun just rising in the sky,
The waking birdlings as they fly,
The grass all wet with morning dew
Are telling me I've just met You!

*From the rising of the sun to its setting
the name of the LORD is to be praised!*
PSALM 113:3

How often do you get to spend time enjoying the
outdoors or taking a walk? Let your stress fly away
and be thankful for the exercise.

---

*I'm grateful for outdoor life, Lord—birds singing,
clouds hovering, leaves waving in the breeze.
I feel as if I've met You all over again each time
I spend time in Your vast creation. From the
moment the sun splits the night sky until the
second it disappears out of view, I'm reminded
at every turn. You're there, Lord. Let all of
creation sing Your praise. You're there! Amen.*

Day 203

REACHING OUT

Today my soul is reaching out
for something that's unknown,
I cannot grasp or fathom it,
for it's known to God alone.

Is there a thing of which it is said, "See, this is new"?
It has been already, in the ages before us.
ECCLESIASTES 1:10

What would you like God to make known to you?

So many times I just can't put my finger on
what's troubling me, Lord. I'm worried.
Concerned. Troubled. The reason often eludes
me, which causes even more concern. During
these seasons when things are unclear, I choose
to continue to trust that You know everything.
You don't just see my troubles, Father; You see the
solutions. And You're already putting together a plan
to move me in the right direction. I trust
You, Lord. In all things, I trust You. Amen.

Day 204

IT'S ONLY A BEND

We stand at life's crossroads
And view what we think is the end,
But God has a much bigger vision,
And He tells us it's only a bend.

Show me the way I should go,
for to you I entrust my life.
PSALM 143:8 NIV

When you face a bend in the road, how do
you trust that God will see you through it?

I'm grateful for the reminder, Lord, that a bend
in the road isn't the end of the road. You've got plenty
of miles ahead for me, Father. And You're going to
show me, day by day, minute by minute, which way
to walk. I'm grateful for Your "wider vision," because
I know You see everything that is (so far) unseen by
human eyes. I choose to take Your hand and walk
with You, trusting that You know the way. Amen.

A CHEERFUL ATTITUDE

If you'll only try to be cheerful,
You will find, without a doubt,
A cheerful attitude is something
No one should be without.

A cheerful heart is a good medicine.
PROVERBS 17:22

What brings you cheer in the summertime?
What do you find to be cheerful about
in the other seasons of the year?

I need the medicine that a happy heart can bring,
Lord. I've been through enough seasons of sadness.
It's not always easy to remain cheerful and upbeat
when things around me aren't going my way,
but I'm grateful for the reminder that You want
me to try, Father. Today I choose to do just that.
May the smile on my face be a reflection of the
joy in my heart—a joy that can only come
from a relationship with You, Lord. Amen.

Day 206

WRAPPED IN KINDNESS

If you practice kindness
In all you say and do,
The Lord will wrap His kindness
Around your heart and you.

He who pursues righteousness and
kindness will find life and honor.
PROVERBS 21:21

How can you encourage your
husband or children this week?

I want to be known as one who is kindhearted,
Lord. May it come naturally to me. I don't
want to have to force myself to be thoughtful
and kind to others, Father. May the kindness
You've bestowed upon me motivate me to treat
others with the same sweetness. I want to be a
reflection of You. Today I choose to do my very
best to treat others with godly kindness. Amen.

A Prayer for You

Here is a prayer for you
That you'll walk with God every day,
Remembering always in whatever you do,
There is only one true, righteous way.

*"And I will walk among you, and will
be your God, and you shall be my people."*
Leviticus 26:12

Do you know of someone who needs
a closer relationship with the Lord?
Pray for that person today.

---

*This world is filled with troubled, confused people,
Lord. They all have different ideas about how
to get to heaven. Some want to work their way
there. Others choose to follow false gods. My heart,
my prayer, is for all to come to know You, Lord.
May I shine my light in such a way that others
will be drawn to Your Word, that they might
know the one true path to eternal life,
through Jesus Christ. Amen.*

MY CATHEDRAL

My garden beautifies my yard
and adds fragrance to the air,
But it is also my cathedral
and my quiet place of prayer.

And they heard the sound of the LORD
God walking in the garden in the cool of the day.
GENESIS 3:8

Where in God's creation do
you find inspiration? Why?

There's such peace, such joy, in Your creation, Lord!
When I look at the buds of a flower bursting
forth in their fullness, when I smell the aroma
of a blossoming rose, my heart is overflowing
with wonder and appreciation. Each petal is a
reminder that You are the Author of all, that You
created every living thing for my pleasure, my joy.
May I never forget that Your love for me can
be found all around me, Father. Amen.

Day 209

WALK IN LOVE

Love changes darkness into light
And makes the heart take wingless flight—
Oh, blessed are they who walk in love,
They also walk with God above.

Love bears all things, believes all things,
hopes all things, endures all things.
1 CORINTHIANS 13:7

Whom can you touch with God's comfort today?

I have walked through seasons of great
burdens, Lord, when my heart felt as though
it were made of stone. I'm so grateful for Your
great love, which turned my darkness into light
and reminded me that my heart could be as light
as a feather if I would only turn my problems
over to You. Your love for me is so vast, Father.
You've blessed me above all I could ask or imagine.
Praise You for the changes Your love has
made to my heart, Lord. Amen.

A Heaven-Sent Gift

Happiness is giving up thoughts
That breed discontent
And accepting what comes
As a gift heaven sent.

He who gives heed to the word will prosper,
and happy is he who trusts in the LORD.
PROVERBS 16:20

What thoughts of discontent
do you need to give up today?

I'll admit it, Lord: I've walked through seasons
of discontentment. I've refused to see the good and
instead chosen to hone in on the things that didn't
satisfy or fulfill me. Forgive me, Father, for focusing
only on myself—my wants, wishes, and desires.
May I seek to please Your heart, Lord, not my own.
May I be God-focused first, others-focused second,
and, finally, content to enjoy the work You are
doing in my heart as a result. Amen.

Day 211

Trust Him

Deal only with the present
Never step into tomorrow,
For God asks us just to trust in Him
And to never borrow sorrow.

*Yea, our heart is glad in him, because
we trust in his holy name.*
PSALM 33:21

How can you train yourself to
take on life one day at a time?

---

*So many times, Lord, I've borrowed sorrow
from tomorrow. I've skipped ahead a day or
two—or ten or twelve—and projected fear on
my situation. You ask me to live for today, Father,
and I will give it my best shot, but I definitely need
Your help. Help me to remember that You've only
given me enough grace to get through this one day.
I choose to do so with my hand in Yours, Lord. Amen.*

Day 212

TIME TO BE KIND

In this troubled world it's
refreshing to find
Someone who still has
the time to be kind.

*Always strive to do what is good for
each other and for everyone else.*
1 THESSALONIANS 5:15 NIV

How can you be a witness to the unsaved today?

---

*All around me, Lord, there are people in pain.
They're going through struggles I will never know
about. Many are just looking for a friend, someone
with a kind word, a smile, a thoughtful gesture.
May I be that someone to others in pain, Father.
I want to do what is good for others. Thank You
for the reminder that many people are just one
friendship away from getting to know You, Lord.
May I be that sort of friend. Amen.*

WALK WITH COURAGE

Be glad that you've walked
With courage each day—
Be glad you've had strength
For each step of the way.

Keep steady my steps according to thy promise,
and let no iniquity get dominion over me.
PSALM 119:133

How can you cultivate an atmosphere
of dependence on God in your home?

My shoulders are squared, Lord. My stance is set.
My hand is firmly clutching Yours. Today, as I face
the Goliaths in front of me, I ask for Your courage,
Your tenacity, Your assistance. I know that any
strength inside of me comes straight from You,
so I remain dependent on You. No showing off here,
Lord. It's all You, Father! I choose to trust You
to fight my battles for me today. Amen.

Day 214

HAPPY MEMORIES

Memories are treasures
Time cannot take away,
So may you be surrounded
By happy ones today.

I thank my God every time I remember you.
PHILIPPIANS 1:3 NIV

What treasured memories spring to mind
today? Take the time to thank God for those
joyous times in the past and the memories
you will make tomorrow.

---

*Sometimes memories flood over me from out of
nowhere, Lord. I don't see them coming. They
sweep over me, like ocean waves, reminding me
of days of old. Thank You for the experiences I've
had so far, Father, even the tough ones. Your healing
balm has brought me through some rough times.
Now, when I look back, I see with twenty-twenty
perspective. You've made beauty from ashes,
Father, and I'm so thankful. Amen.*

Day 215

AS FOR ME AND MY HOUSE

What a treasure house filled with rare jewels
Are the blessings of year upon year,
When life has been lived as you've lived it
In a home where God's presence is near.

For through wisdom your days will be many,
and years will be added to your life.
PROVERBS 9:11 NIV

How can you rejoice in God's presence today?

Sometimes I feel like my life is a box filled with
precious jewels, Father! You've gifted me with
friends who are like diamonds. You've surrounded
me with blessings—a good job, a home, food, and
more. Each blessing shimmers and shines. Your love
is the key that opens this treasure-filled box, Father.
I'm so grateful that You've sent such lovely gifts
my way! I'm grateful for every jewel! Amen.

Day 216

JOURNEY ON

Never give up and never stop—
Just journey on to the mountaintop.

*If I have all faith, so as to remove mountains,
but have not love, I am nothing.*
1 CORINTHIANS 13:2

How does God provide you with
strength when you are weary?

---

*I don't journey from valley to valley, Lord.
Instead, I move from peak to peak. May I be
encouraged by the highs and grow from the lows.
No matter where life takes me—be it valley or
peak—I refuse to give up. Instead, I look to You,
Father. You're right there, lifting me over hurdles,
giving me strength to keep trekking, even when
I'm exhausted. My faith is strong today, Lord.
With You, this journey will be amazing. Amen.*

Day 217

ASK IN FAITH

There's no problem too big
And no question too small,
Just ask God in faith
And He'll answer them all.

Commit your work to the LORD,
and your plans will be established.
PROVERBS 16:3

What work have you committed to the Lord?

Sometimes I focus on the extremes, Lord—
the high highs and low lows. I get so caught up
in the exaggerated seasons that I forget to trust
You. There's truly no problem too big for You,
Father. I can take any woe to Your throne. Increase
my faith today, I pray, so I truly believe You will
move on my behalf, even when the mountain in front
of me seems immovable. I trust You, Lord. Amen.

ANGELS ALL AROUND

On life's busy thoroughfares
We meet with angels unawares—
Often we're too busy to listen or hear,
Too busy to sense that God is near.

*"Truly, I say to you, as you did it not to
one of the least of these, you did it not to me."*
MATTHEW 25:45

How do you see God in your immediate family?
At work? At church?

*Everywhere I look, Father, You are there! I see You
in the eyes of a child. I catch a glimpse of You in the
homeless man on the street. I'm reminded of Your
great love when I watch a little one at play with
her father. I'm blissfully overwhelmed when earthly
romance reminds me of Your great love for me,
Your bride. In short, Father, I see You all around me,
and I love what I see. Thank You for the daily
reminders that You're right here, Lord. Amen.*

THANKS FOR THE LITTLE THINGS

Thank You, God, for little things
That often come our way—
The things we take for granted
But don't mention when we pray.

*Better is a little with righteousness
than great revenues with injustice.*
PROVERBS 16:8

How can you make a conscious effort to thank
God for His smallest blessings every day?

---

*How many miracles did I fail to notice today, Lord?
How many blessings? How many answered prayers?
How many healings of the heart, mind, or body did I
overlook? Tune my ears to hear, Lord. Focus my eyes
to see. I don't want to miss a thing, Father, for You
are on the move all around me. May nothing escape
my attention, for every miracle, no matter how
small, is worthy of praise. Thank You, Father. Amen.*

Day 220

TEARS TO SMILES

God is our encouragement
In trouble and in trials,
And in suffering and in sorrow
He will turn our tears to smiles.

May the God of steadfastness and encouragement
grant you to live in such harmony with one
another, in accord with Christ Jesus.
ROMANS 15:5

Imagine yourself in God's arms.
How is He holding you?

Sometimes my tears flow with such anguish, Lord,
that I wonder if I will ever smile again. On those
days, I curl up in a ball, Your arms wrapped tightly
around me. What an Encourager You are, Father.
You whisper, "Peace, be still," and lift my spirits. You
turn my tears to a smile, my suffering and sorrow
to joy. No one loves me the way You do, Father.
I'm so grateful for the way You pour out love
and compassion on me, Your child. Amen.

UNEXPECTED JOYS

Thank You, God, for little
things that come unexpectedly
To brighten up a dreary day
that dawned so dismally.

*It is good to give thanks to the LORD, to sing praises to
thy name, O Most High; to declare thy steadfast love
in the morning, and thy faithfulness by night.*
PSALM 92:1–2

How have you experienced an unexpected
joy recently? What can you do to surprise
someone else with a similar blessing?

---

*I don't always get off to a strong start, Lord, but I
want to be a woman who finishes well. No matter
how rocky the beginning of each day might be, I
want to shift my focus to You so I'll end up closer to
You at the end of the day than ever before. Today I
choose to praise You, Father, and to draw near. Your
steadfast love holds me tight, no matter what I'm
facing. I'm ever thankful, Lord. Amen.*

WARM OUR HEARTS

Oh, God, who made the summer
And warmed the earth with beauty,
Warm our hearts with gratitude
And devotion to our duty.

Enter his gates with thanksgiving, and his courts
with praise! Give thanks to him, bless his name!
PSALM 100:4

What work do you see as a duty?
How can you be thankful for it anyway?

Lord, may I be ever grateful, even when my
workload is heavy, even when the "duties" of this life
seem too much to bear. I'm grateful for the things You
entrust to my care, Father. You're growing me into
a woman You're very proud of, and that makes my
heart happy. May I have a heart of thanksgiving
today and all my days to come, Father. Amen.

SUNSHINE AND JOY

Thank You, God, for brushing
the dark clouds from my mind
And leaving only sunshine
and joy of heart behind.

Thy testimonies are my heritage for ever;
yea, they are the joy of my heart.
PSALM 119:111

What Bible verse can you plant in your
heart as a shield against loneliness?

There have been times, Lord, when loneliness
has wrapped itself around my heart like a dismal
cloud I couldn't see past. During those seasons
You've swept in like only You could—adding sunlight,
quickening my heart, bringing hope where there
was none. I'm overwhelmed at how much You care,
Father. . .how much You adore me. Where would I
be without You? I praise You for the transforming
work You're doing in my life. Amen.

JOYOUS ACCEPTANCE

Make us conscious that Your
love comes in many ways
And not always just as happiness
and bright and shining days. . .
Often You send trouble
and we foolishly reject it,
Not realizing that it is Your will
and we should joyously accept it.

He who spares the rod hates his son, but he
who loves him is diligent to discipline him.
PROVERBS 13:24

When has foolishness on your part been a detriment?
How did you overcome such foolishness?

I haven't always made the best decisions, Lord. I've
made plenty of mistakes along the way. Still, You
forgive. You inch me forward. . .Your plans for my
life always bringing hope. I've learned so much
during seasons of discipline, Father. Best of all, I've
grown to love and trust You more. Thank You for
taking the time to grow me into a woman of faith,
someone You can use to reach others. Amen.

Day 225

STRONG FAITH, TRUE PURPOSE

Nothing is ever too hard to do
If your faith is strong and
your purpose is true.

But Jesus looked at them and said to them, "With men
this is impossible, but with God all things are possible."
MATTHEW 19:26

What are the most difficult situations
you are facing? How has your faith
in Christ helped you already?

How many times have I used the words "This
is impossible," Lord? Too many to count! I get
overwhelmed when I face the mountains in my
life and often give up before I even give faith a
try. Thank You for the reminder that with You
nothing is impossible. No mountain is too big.
Increase my faith, I pray. May I see with Your eyes,
so that mountains can disappear into the sea! Amen.

Day 226

Mustard-Seed Faith

All we really ever need
Is faith as a grain of a mustard seed,
For all God asks is, "Do you believe?"
For if you do ye shall receive.

"For truly, I say to you, if you have faith as
a grain of mustard seed, you will say to this
mountain, 'Move from here to there,' and it will
move; and nothing will be impossible to you."
MATTHEW 17:20

How have you grown spiritually this year?
Are you closer to God or farther away from Him?

My faith feels so small at times, Lord. I wonder
if I can accomplish anything at all. Then I'm
reminded that You aren't looking for massive
faith. Your Word says it only takes a little. So, I
take that tiny mustard-seed faith and apply it to
the challenges I'm facing today, Lord. With Your
help, nothing is impossible. Take my faith and
do great and mighty things, I pray. Amen.

SERVICE

Great is our gladness
To serve God through others,
For our Father taught us that
All women are sisters and all men are brothers.

*"So whatever you wish that men would do to you,
do so to them; for this is the law and the prophets."*
MATTHEW 7:12

Do you know someone who often serves others? Find
a way to serve that person today.

---

*Open my eyes to those around me, Lord. Who do
You want me to serve today? Who can I bless?
Speak specifically, Lord, that I might impact the
life of someone who needs an extra touch of
kindness. Point me in the direction of one who
needs hope, love, courage. . . . Then give me
whatever it takes to be Your hands, Your feet
to the one in need. Serving others is so much
fun, Lord. Thanks for using me. Amen.*

Day 228

KEEP ON BELIEVING

Remember, there's no cloud too dark
For God's light to penetrate
If we keep on believing
And have faith enough to wait!

When I sit in darkness, the LORD will be a light to me.
MICAH 7:8

Do you struggle with anxiety? How does
the Lord provide you with light and
peace during those times?

---

*I've never been very good at waiting, Lord.
I want things to change. . .now. I want the
light to break through the darkness, penetrating
the forces of evil, that I might walk in hope.
While I'm waiting, Father, fill me with hope.
May I never forget that You're already on the
move, no matter what things look like on the
surface. Give me peace until I can see the
daylight break through, Lord. Amen.*

BOUNTIFUL GIFTS

More than hearts can imagine
or minds comprehend,
God's bountiful gifts are
ours without end.

The LORD loves righteousness and justice;
the earth is full of his unfailing love.
PSALM 33:5 NIV

When have you been given the gift of a smile?
Of a hug or a kiss? Of a blessing?

Bountiful. *How I love that word, Lord. You don't*
just bless me. You go above and beyond all I could ask
or think, offering bountiful, overflowing blessings.
That's how much You love me. I can't comprehend
such love, Father, but I want to overflow with it,
as You do. May I learn to bless others in the same
surprising, blissful way, that they might see Your
heart in all I do. How I love You, Lord. Amen.

Day 230

EVERY GOOD GIFT

Thank You, God, for everything—
The big things and the small,
For every good gift comes from God—
The Giver of them all.

*For from him and through him and to him
are all things. To him be glory for ever.*
ROMANS 11:36

Are you a good gift giver? How does giving good
gifts to others make you feel? How can you
relate this to your relationship with God?

---

*How I love to give gifts, Father. I know I get this
trait from You, for You are the best Gift Giver ever.
I see Your hand at work, giving the gifts of hope, life,
joy, peace, and a thousand others. Every day brings
more good things from Your generous hand. These
gifts aren't wrapped up in ribbons and bows, but
they're some of the finest I've ever received, Father,
and I'm so grateful for them. Thank You! Amen.*

A PEACEFUL ISLE

God's love is like an island
In life's ocean, vast and wide—
A peaceful, quiet shelter
From the restless, rising tide!

"I would haste to find me a shelter
from the raging wind and tempest."
PSALM 55:8

How has God's love and care
brought you peace in the past?

Thank You, Lord, for giving me a peaceful place
to rest in You. Life can be so exhausting. I get
weary going from place to place at such a rapid pace.
Just keeping up with the bills, the kids, the job
. . .it can all be so overwhelming. But, Father, You
provide an island of love and peace, a special place
where You long to meet with me for some one-on-
one time. I need the comfort that only You can bring.
Thank You for the shelter You provide. Amen.

Day 232

A SINCERE HEART

God is always listening to hear
Prayers that are made by a
heart that's sincere.

For everything created by God is good, and nothing
is to be rejected if it is received with thanksgiving;
for then it is consecrated by the word of God and prayer.
1 TIMOTHY 4:4–5

Which of your friends need some prayer today?

_____

Father, I long to spend more time with You,
to pray in earnest for others. Don't let another
moment slip by without nudging me to pray.
Shift my focus from self to others. May I never
forget that time spent interceding for others is
well spent, indeed. Give me a passion for the lost
and for those in great need, I pray. Thank You,
Lord, for growing my prayer life. Amen.

Hearts and Minds

There's something we should not forget—
That the people we've known,
or heard of, or met
By indirection have had a big part
In molding the thoughts of
the mind and the heart.

*A man's mind plans his way,
but the Lord directs his steps.*
Proverbs 16:9

Who in your life started out as a
stranger or acquaintance but has now
impacted you in a surprising way?

---

*Lord, today I thank You for every person
who has directly—or indirectly—affected my
growth as a Christian. Those who've poured
into my life. Those who've challenged me.
Those who've motivated and inspired. For all of
these people I'm thankful, Father, for they have
molded me into the woman of God I have become.
I'm grateful for each and every one, Lord. Amen.*

HE IS GREATER

Whatever we ask for
Falls short of God's giving,
For His greatness exceeds
Every facet of living.

Great is the LORD, and greatly to be praised,
and his greatness is unsearchable.
PSALM 145:3

What are your concerns about monetary matters?
How have you seen God's generosity in the past?

No matter how much I give, Lord—be it
money or time or effort—Your giving far exceeds
my own. May I learn from Your example of
generosity. May others see me as a giver. Relieve
any anxieties, and free me up to give above and
beyond what I'm now able to offer. May I be a
woman who goes above and beyond with her
time, talents, and treasures, Lord. Amen.

PRAYER IS NOT. . .

Prayers are not meant for obtaining
What we selfishly wish to acquire
For God in His wisdom refuses
The things that we wrongly desire.

When I think of thy ordinances
from of old, I take comfort, O LORD.
PSALM 119:52

When has God said no to your prayers before?
When has He said yes?

Not all of Your answers to my prayers have been
"yes," Lord. There have been some difficult "nos"
along the way. And though I didn't necessarily
understand Your answers at the time, I've learned
from each one. I've learned to trust You more during
the "no" seasons, Lord, and I've learned patience
as well. And while it hasn't always been easy, I'm
still grateful that You haven't always said yes. I'm
thankful You're growing me into a woman who trusts
You, even when I don't get what I want. Amen.

Day 236

A DAILY GUEST

Every home
Is specially blessed
When God becomes
A daily guest.

May God be gracious to us and bless us
and make his face to shine upon us.
PSALM 67:1

What is in your home that shows
visitors your love for God?

Lord, You will always be the guest of honor in my
home. I promise to make room for You, day or night,
whenever You desire to spend time with me. My
door will be unlocked. I'll have the teakettle on,
ready to fill my cup so I can settle in for a cozy
conversation with You, my Best Friend. Thank
You for knocking on my heart's door, Father.
I love our time together. Amen.

LAWS TO LIVE BY

Let nothing sway you
Or turn you away
From God's old commandments—
They are still new today.

Praise the LORD! Blessed is the man who fears the LORD,
who greatly delights in his commandments!
PSALM 112:1

How do you find delight in the laws of the Lord?
Are they just a list of rules to you, or do they mean
more? How did Jesus change the bondage of Old
Testament law, and how is it still the same?

Thank You for writing Your laws upon my
heart, Father. I'm so glad they're not simply a
list of dos and don'ts, but, rather, a part of who
I am as Your child. You've given them to me for
my safety, my provision, my joy. Today I choose
to delight in Your Word, Father. May I live
within the boundaries You have set, that
all will go well with me. Amen.

STRONG SPIRITS

Whenever we are troubled
And life has lost its song,
It's God testing us with burdens
Just to make our spirits strong!

This is my comfort in my affliction
that thy promise gives me life.
PSALM 119:50

How has God worked through
your times of trial in the past?

I've faced trials, Lord, and have learned many
lessons as a result. There have been days when
it was hard to find my voice, let alone sing a
song of praise. During those seasons, You've always
brought comfort. And I know You'll do the same
in the future, Father. No matter what comes my
way—pleasure or pain—I know I can trust You.
You've promised this in Your Word, and I know
I can hang tight to Your promises. Amen.

Day 239

UNFAILING MEDICATION

When you're feeling downcast,
Seek God in meditation,
For a little talk with Jesus
Is unfailing medication.

I find my delight in thy commandments,
which I love. . .I will meditate on thy statutes.
PSALM 119:47–48

What steps can you take to change
your negative thoughts to positive ones?

Spending time with You is a balm to my soul,
Lord. It soothes, comforts, coats, rebuilds, renews,
and brings healing. Whenever my eyes are downcast,
whenever I'm ready to give up, turning to You is
the answer. There's never been a time when You've
let me down, Father; so I choose to run into Your
arms today. Take my downcast expression and
change it to one of joy, I pray. Amen.

Day 240

A Meditation Hour

So we may know God better
And feel His quiet power,
Let us daily keep in silence
A meditation hour.

Let the words of my mouth and the meditation
of my heart be acceptable in thy sight,
O LORD, my rock and my redeemer.
PSALM 19:14

What is the best time of day to have your devotions
or quiet time? How do you feel if you miss a day?

There's so much power in Your presence, Lord.
It's tangible. I can feel it. I come to You at my
lowest point, zapped of strength. In Your presence
I find not only fullness of joy but overwhelming
strength too. You truly are my rock, Father. You're
the One I cling to. So I come to You again today,
Lord. May I know You more and more as I
spend quiet, refreshing time with You. Amen.

Day 241

A Baby Is...

A baby is a gift of life
Born of the wonder of love—
A little bit of eternity,
Sent from the Father above.

*Lo, sons are a heritage from the LORD,
the fruit of the womb a reward.*
PSALM 127:3

How is God's love different from human love?

---

*What a beautiful gift human life is, Lord!
There's something so miraculous about a newborn
baby. I'm reminded of Your great love for us every
time I gaze into a baby's precious eyes. Today I
praise You for every baby in my circle—children,
grandchildren, nieces, nephews, children of
friends. . .Bless each one, I pray. May they all
grow up to love and follow You. Amen.*

Day 242

GIVE JOY

Time is not measured
By the years that you live,
But by the deeds that you do
And the joy that you give.

Those who devise good meet loyalty and faithfulness.
PROVERBS 14:22

What deeds have you done recently
that have given joy to others?

---

*When I look at all of the days of my life, Lord, I won't
count them in years. Instead, I'll consider them from
joy to joy. I don't know the number of my days (and
I'm glad about that), but every moment is in Your
hands. May I spend each one in communion with
You and in fellowship with those You have placed
around me. Thank You for my life, Father. Amen.*

LIFE ABUNDANT

The more you do unselfishly,
The more you live abundantly. . .
The more of everything you share,
The more you'll always have to spare.

*O LORD, my heart is not lifted up, my eyes are
not raised too high; I do not occupy myself with
things too great and too marvelous for me.*
PSALM 131:1

We are mirrors of Christ—His ambassadors.
How does the world respond to Him
through seeing your actions and deeds?

*I love the concept of unselfish living, Lord.
I want to be an "abundant" woman of God,
one who gives unselfishly—not so I can have
an abundant life; I already have that. But so
I'll always have more to spare, Father. As Your
ambassador, I want to be freed up to give to
those in need, both near and far. May my giving
be a reflection of Your heart, Lord. Amen.*

THINK ON GOD

Through a happy springtime
And a summer filled with love
May we walk into the autumn
With our thoughts on God above.

A cheerful heart is a good medicine,
but a downcast spirit dries up the bones.
PROVERBS 17:22

Which season tends to be the
hardest for you? How can you
focus on the Lord to get through?

I love the seasons You've created, Father. They are
filled with a kaleidoscope of color and bring such
wonder. May I be a woman who transitions easily
through the literal and symbolic seasons of life. I don't
want to be dragged from one to the next, kicking
and screaming. With You I can trust every change,
even when autumn—with all its colorful promises—
morphs into winter's cold. You are faithful, God. Amen.

GOODNESS AND MERCY

Not money or gifts or material things
But understanding and the joy that it brings
Can change this old world and its selfish ways
And put goodness and mercy
back into our days.

By wisdom a house is built, and by understanding
it is established; by knowledge the rooms are
filled with all precious and pleasant riches.
PROVERBS 24:3–4

Who is in charge of the finances in your
household? Can you find ways to cut back
and give the money to a needful cause?

Lord, even if I had all the money in the world,
I couldn't change the culture around me. Only
prayer can make a difference. Well, prayer and
Your mighty hand at work, changing lives,
opinions, thoughts, and actions. Instead of trying
to change others, Father, help me to be a light
in the darkness, that others will feel loved,
not judged. I want to shine bright for You. Amen.

Day 246

GOD LEADS YOU

Instead of just idle supposing,
Step forward to meet each new day
Secure in the knowledge God's near you
To lead you each step of the way.

When you walk, your step will not be hampered;
and if you run, you will not stumble.
PROVERBS 4:12

Imagine yourself holding God's hand.
Where is He leading you?

I'm confident You are at work in my life today, Lord.
I sense Your hand in everything I do. I don't have to
worry or wonder, as long as I follow hard after You,
Father. You've got places for me to go and fantastic
people for me to meet. My steps are ordered by You,
and I won't stumble or fall as long as my hand
remains tightly clutched to Yours. Amen.

BUNDLED TROUBLES

Whenever I am troubled
And lost in deep despair,
I bundle all my troubles up
And go to God in prayer.

He will regard the prayer of the destitute,
and will not despise their supplication.
PSALM 102:17

Why is it so difficult to wait for God's
answers—or to wait at all?

I love the word picture that comes to mind when
I hear the phrase "bundling my troubles" and
bringing them to You, Lord. When my troubles are
bundled, I'm not focused on them. They're not teasing
or taunting me. Instead, they're wrapped tight in
Your protective cocoon. Today, as I place my burdens
at Your feet, I ask that You work through the details,
miraculously solving each problem. I never have
to worry, as long as my problems are in Your
hands and not my own, Lord. Amen.

A HAVEN OF LOVE

God's love is like a beacon
Burning bright with faith and prayer,
And through the changing scenes of life
We can find a haven there!

*Then they were glad because they had quiet,
and he brought them to their desired haven.*
PSALM 107:30

What Bible verse can you set in your
heart as a shield against worry?

---

*The world is looking for hope, Lord. People glance
out over the vast seas and witness tumultuous
waves. Many struggle to survive emotionally
(and even physically). But Your love serves as a
lighthouse, Lord. . .a beacon of hope. People see it
and rush to the safety of Your shore, where they can
find rest and peace. May I be a reflection of that
light today to everyone I meet, Father. Amen.*

Day 249

GOD'S PREFERENCE

When someone does a kindness,
It always seems to me
That's the way God up in heaven
Would like us all to be.

*Teach me thy way, O LORD, that I may walk
in thy truth; unite my heart to fear thy name.*
PSALM 86:11

In what ways can you demonstrate
kindness to others or to yourself?

---

*Random acts of kindness are so fun, Lord. It's a
delight to surprise others with unexpected blessings,
in part because it turns my focus to those around me
but also because it stirs my creativity and helps me to
think like You do. Today, show me how I can express
kindness in a supernatural way to someone I meet
along my path. I want to tap into Your creativity to
bless a friend or loved one today, Lord. Amen.*

WITHDRAW IN PRAYER

When life becomes a problem
Much too great for you to bear,
Instead of trying to escape,
Just withdraw in prayer.

Many are the afflictions of the righteous;
but the LORD delivers him out of them all.
PSALM 34:19

In prayer, do you approach God reverently or
casually? Is this how you think of and treat
God also? Do you need to make a change?

I'll admit it, Lord—many times I want to run
away from my problems. I want to turn on my
heels and flee the room to escape the anguish I
feel. Thank You for the reminder that I don't
have to run and hide. I simply need to withdraw
in prayer and hand my problems over to You.
There's nothing too big for You to handle, Father.
So, I'll stay put. No running for me. Amen.

GIFTS FROM THE HEART

With our hands we give gifts
that money cannot buy.
Diamonds that sparkle
like stars in the sky,
But only the heart can give away
The gift of peace and a perfect day.

May the LORD give strength to his people!
May the LORD bless his people with peace!
PSALM 29:11

Can you describe the difference between
the peace of God and peace with God?

---

*I'm so glad You give the kind of gifts that really
matter, Lord—peace, joy, patience, love, and more.
These presents make an eternal difference. And best
of all, I don't need to write a big check to acquire
Your special gifts; they come free of charge when
I enter into a relationship with You. Thank You
for caring enough to bless me with the things
that matter, Lord. I'm so grateful. Amen.*

Day 252

LOVELY MIRACLES

God sends His little angels
In many forms and guises,
They come as lovely miracles
That God alone devises.

Thy hands have made and fashioned me; give me
understanding that I may learn thy commandments.
PSALM 119:73

What can you learn from people who are different
from you? What characteristics do you see in them?

I love that Your kids are so unique, Lord. They're not
all cookie-cutter. Your family is made up of billions
of people across the globe in every color, size, and
shape—each one loved by You. Thank You for the
miracle of individuality. Each person You've created
is a miracle, and each was made to impact the world
differently. May I never resent our differences,
Father. Instead, I want to celebrate them! Amen.

Day 253

I NEED PEACE

"Thou wilt keep him in perfect peace
Whose mind is stayed on thee."
And, God, if anyone needs peace,
It certainly is me!

A man's spirit will endure sickness;
but a broken spirit who can bear?
PROVERBS 18:14

Do you need to get rid of some
bitterness in your life right now?

Hanging on to bitterness is a real problem for me
at times, Lord. My fingers cling to it, as though it
offers life instead of death. Today I release my hold.
I lay my frustrations, all bitterness, all unforgiveness
at Your feet. Holding on doesn't do me a bit of good,
Father. In fact, it holds me back. So, I choose to let
go, knowing that You can bring the peace I need
to move forward. Thank You, Lord. Amen.

Day 254

GOD LOVES YOU STILL

Somebody cares and always will,
The world forgets but God loves you still.
You cannot go beyond His love
No matter what you're guilty of.

For thou, O Lord, art good and forgiving,
abounding in steadfast love to all who call on thee.
PSALM 86:5

Do you struggle with guilt? Do you need to
ask for the Lord's forgiveness, or is Satan
simply using this feeling to keep you down?

Sometimes guilt weighs me down, Lord. I know
You're ready and willing to forgive my sins, but
confessing them isn't always easy. Today I bring
everything to You—all transgressions big and
small—and ask for a chance to begin anew. Please
forgive me, Father, for anything that has broken
Your heart. I long to walk in forgiveness and peace
once more, so I'm trusting in Your willingness
to release me from the past. Amen.

HE NEVER FORSAKES

The seasons swiftly come and go
and with them comes the thought
Of all the various changes that
time in its flight has brought,
But one thing never changes,
it remains the same forever,
God truly loves His children
and He will forsake them never!

*Hide not thy face from me. Turn not thy servant away
in anger, thou who hast been my help. Cast me not off,
forsake me not, O God of my salvation!*
PSALM 27:9

What are some of the ways
God shows His love for us?

---

*Sometimes the seasons buzz by so quickly, Lord,
that they barely leave an impression. Your love, on
the other hand, sticks with me forever. It's more than
just a blip on my radar—it's life-changing! So, while
this world is spinning around me, while seasons come
and go, I remain rooted and grounded in the truth
that Your love will last for all eternity. Amen.*

Day 256

A RICH REWARD

The love you give to others
Is returned to you by the Lord. . .
And the love of God
Is your soul's rich reward.

*One man gives freely, yet grows all the richer; another
withholds what he should give, and only suffers want.*
PROVERBS 11:24

How can you cultivate an atmosphere
of love in your home?

---

*The rewards You send my way are like a
treasure chest, Lord. I open it to discover
amazing gifts, straight from Your hand. Best of
all, these gifts are meant to be shared with those
I come in contact with. When I share gifts like
peace, love, and joy, You multiply them and send
them back my way. There's no losing with You,
Father. You're the best Gift Giver ever! Amen.*

TENDER MEMORIES

Tender little memories
Of some word or deed
Give us strength and courage
When we are in need.

*The righteous will never be moved;
he will be remembered for ever.*
PSALM 112:6

When have someone's words encouraged you?
What did he or she say?

---

*There are days when I feel left out. Lost. Lonely.
Then a memory washes over me. I remember a kind
word spoken by a friend. I'm reminded of a gift
given by a loved one. I think back to a day when You
came through for me in a special way. I love those
memories, Lord, for they serve as reminders that I'm
never forgotten or overlooked. You care about my
feelings. Thank You. I love You, Lord. Amen.*

THE FATHER'S PROTECTION

Remember God loves you
And wants to protect you,
So seek that small haven
And be guided by prayer
To that place of protection
Within God's loving care.

*"Every word of God is flawless; he is a shield
to those who take refuge in him."*
PROVERBS 30:5 NIV

When do you need a safe place to rest?

---

*There are days when I need a safe haven, Lord,
a place to hide away from the troubles of this
world. Your Word says that You cover me with
Your wing. I love that image, Father! Today I
choose to curl up in that safe place so that healing
and peace can take the place of the turmoil in
my heart. Thank You for proving a safe haven,
Lord. I love spending time with You! Amen.*

MORNING, NOON, AND NIGHT

Meet God in the morning
And go with Him through the day
And thank Him for His guidance
Each evening when you pray.

*O LORD, in the morning thou dost hear my voice; in
the morning I prepare a sacrifice for thee, and watch.*
PSALM 5:3

How has God guided your life so far?

---

*You're an all-day-long leader, Father. In the
morning when I wake, You're right there,
giving me guidance for the day ahead. Hours
later, You're still there, calming me down when
my workload seems too great. And at night,
You tuck me in, Your presence so real to me as I
drift off to sleep. I'm so thankful for Your daily
provision and protection, Lord! Amen.*

PATIENCE AND CONTENTMENT

Teach me to be patient
In everything I do,
Content to trust Your wisdom
And to follow after You.

*Fret not yourself because of evildoers, and be not
envious of the wicked; for the evil man has no
future; the lamp of the wicked will be put out.*
PROVERBS 24:19–20

Are you content with God, your husband,
your children, your home, your job?
In what areas are you discontent?

---

*Forgive me for the many times I've expressed
discontentment, Father! You've taken such good
care of me and provided for every need. May I
have an attitude of gratitude so that contentment
reigns in my heart. You're such a loving and giving
Father. May I never forget how beautifully You've
taken care of me. I love You, Lord. Amen.*

Day 261

HIGHER GOALS

Father up in heaven,
Stir and wake our sleeping souls,
Renew our faith and lift us up
And give us higher goals.

*I press on toward the goal to win the prize for which
God has called me heavenward in Christ Jesus.*
PHILIPPIANS 3:14 NIV

What are some of your goals for the next five years?

---

*I want to be a goal setter, Lord. I want to view
the future with great hope. Help me set clear,
realistic goals so that I can begin to take steps in
the direction You've called me. May I remain
diligent as I move forward, undeterred by any
obstacles in my way. Awaken me, I pray,
and give clear direction, Father. Amen.*

SHOW LOVE TO ALL

To be peaceful, I must be kind
For peace can't exist in a hate-torn mind,
So to have peace I must always show
Love to all people I meet, see, or know.

He who respects the commandment will be rewarded.
PROVERBS 13:13

What steals joy and peace from your heart?
How can you combat these issues?

*I'll admit it: some people are harder to love
than others, Lord. They grate on my nerves and
cause frustration. Thank You for the reminder
that I'm called to love everyone, even the most
unlovable person. Instead of battling anger or
frustration when I come in contact with these
people, help me to love them as You would. Help
change my heart, Father. Thank You! Amen.*

WORSHIP EVERYWHERE

I have worshipped in churches
and chapels,
I have prayed in the busy street,
I have sought my God and
have found Him
Where the waves of the ocean beat.

O come, let us worship and bow down,
let us kneel before the LORD, our Maker!
PSALM 95:6

Think of a time in your life when God
seemed intimately close to you.
Do you feel the same way today?

I sense Your presence all around me, Lord!
Whether I'm on a crowded street corner or seated
in a cozy chapel, You're right there. Thank You
for the reminder that You want to meet with me,
no matter where I go. I can draw near to You
on a city bus, a country road, or in a majestic
cathedral. You are awesome, my ever-present
God! How I praise You! Amen.

Day 264

PEACE OF SOUL

Only by the grace of God
Can we gain self-control,
And only meditative thoughts
Can restore our peace of soul.

*In peace I will both lie down and sleep; for thou
alone, O LORD, makest me dwell in safety.*
PSALM 4:8

In what past situations should
you have prayed for self-control?

---

*I don't always exhibit self-control, Father.
Sometimes I eat too much, say too much, demand
too much. . . . It's easy to point out the flaws
in others, but I don't always recognize lack of
self-control in myself. Today I confess it to You.
Please intervene and give me the control I need,
so that I can live a more peaceful, contented life.
I want to be a good example to others and to
experience true peace in my soul. I need
Your help, Lord. Amen.*

Day 265

GOD'S GOODNESS PREVAILS

Wait with a heart that is patient
For the goodness of God to prevail,
For never do our prayers go unanswered,
And His mercy and love never fail.

Be still before the LORD, and wait patiently for him.
PSALM 37:7

Do you ever feel that your prayers go
unanswered? How do you feel when
others' prayers are answered?

---

*Your answers come on Your timetable, Lord. I'm
learning this as I grow in my faith. There's a lot
of waiting at times, but You're teaching me to be
patient and hopeful, even when I can't see what's
coming around the next bend. Today I choose to
remain still in Your presence, content and filled
with hope for what I know You're about to do.
You've got this, Lord. I can trust You. Amen.*

IT'S A WONDERFUL WORLD

God is so lavish in all that He's done
To make this great world
such a wonderful one. . .
His mountains are high,
His oceans are deep,
And vast and unmeasured
the prairielands sweep.

In his hand are the depths of the earth;
the heights of the mountains are his also.
PSALM 95:4

What part of God's creation
do you find most amazing?

I love the word lavish, *Lord. You heap so many*
good things on us, oftentimes undeserved. You've
given us an amazing planet to live on, yummy
foods to eat, blissful relationships to share. . . . We've
been blessed with starry skies, ocean waves, playful
puppies, giggling babies, and a vast array of other
remarkable blessings. May we never forget that
we're surrounded by Your lavish goodness on
every side. Praise You, Father! Amen.

Searching for a Savior

If you would find the Savior,
No need to search afar—
For God is all around you,
No matter where you are!

You hem me in behind and before,
and you lay your hand upon me.
Psalm 139:5 niv

To whom or what do you go first for comfort?

I love this biblical promise, Lord, that You hem
me in behind and before. If I take a step into
the future, You are there. If I could go back to
yesterday, You would be there too. I don't have
to go searching for Your presence, Father. You're
always with me, in good times and bad. How
can I ever thank You for sticking so close?
I appreciate Your nearness, Lord. Amen.

REPLENISH MY SOUL

It fills me with joy just to linger with You
As my soul You replenish
and my heart You renew,
For prayer is much more
than just asking for things—
It's the peace and contentment
that quietness brings.

*"The LORD your God is in your midst. . .he will rejoice
over you with gladness, he will renew you in his love."*
ZEPHANIAH 3:17

When are you most content?

*I feel so empty at times, Lord. I wonder if
I'll ever have that "full" feeling again. But
then You come near and replenish me! You
take my tank from empty to full with just one
moment in Your presence. I'm overwhelmed
with Your ability to touch my heart so beautifully,
Father. You renew, reinvigorate, and revive. . .
with just a touch. Thank You! Amen.*

Day 269

MY LOVED ONES

Father, hear this little prayer—
Reach across the miles from here to there,
So I can feel much closer to
those I'm fondest of,
And they may know I think of them
with thankfulness and love.

*"Hear my prayer, O LORD, and give ear to my cry;
hold not thy peace at my tears! For I am thy
passing guest, a sojourner, like all my fathers."*
PSALM 39:12

How often do you pray for your family and
friends who live far away? How do you pray
for them? How can you reach out and
let them know you care?

---

*Separation is so hard, Lord. There are times
when I wish I could gather up all of my loved ones,
like a mother hen gathering her chicks, and pull them
close. I'm grateful for modern technology—phones,
video calls, social media, and so on—so that I can
stay in touch with those I love, both near and far.
Best of all, I thank You for the opportunity to pray
for those I'm missing. In those moments, they are
particularly close to my heart, Lord. Amen.*

INFINITE SKY

Each day at dawning
I lift my heart high
And raise up my eyes
To the infinite sky.

*You will do well to pay attention to this as to a
lamp shining in a dark place, until the day dawns
and the morning star rises in your hearts.*
2 PETER 1:19

How are you at giving thanks when trials
come? Can you give thanks for specifics in
the situation even if you aren't happy
about the situation in general?

---

*Each day brings new beginnings, Lord. . .new
chances to start afresh. Today I sense things
stirring in my heart. I lift my head, my heart,
my eyes to focus on You today. I praise You in
advance for the remarkable things You're setting
in motion for me, even now. The possibilities
are endless with You, Father. I look forward
to walking out Your plan for my life. Amen.*

MORE EQUALS LESS

The more you give,
The more you get—
The more you laugh,
The less you fret!

The meek shall possess the land, and delight
themselves in abundant prosperity.
PSALM 37:11

Reflect on a time your own generosity
was returned to you tenfold.

I love Your method of measurement, Lord.
When I give more, I get more. When I let go,
You're free to pile on the blessings. Best of all,
when I choose joy in every circumstance,
I'm released from fretting and anguish.
What a blissful trade-off, Father. I always
come out on the winning side when I
stick with You. Praise You! Amen.

SHINE

Do not sit and idly wish for wider,
new dimensions
Where you can put in practice
your good intentions,
But at the spot God placed you,
begin at once to do
Little things to brighten up
the lives surrounding you.

The path of the righteous is like the light of dawn,
which shines brighter and brighter until full day.
PROVERBS 4:18

Are you following God's will and
what He wants you to be doing?

No more excuses, Lord. No more waiting in the
background for perfect timing and circumstances
before I serve You. Today I choose to take a step
toward the plans You have for my life, even if it's a
struggle. I'll do what I can to make progress and to
brighten the lives of those around me as I go. I ask
for Your help as I take this step, Lord. Amen.

Day 273

THE UNKNOWN

The future is not ours to know,
And it may never be—
So let us live and give our best,
And give it lavishly.

*Let not your heart envy sinners, but continue
in the fear of the LORD all the day. Surely there
is a future, and your hope will not be cut off.*
PROVERBS 23:17–18

Are you looking at the future with
eyes of faith or with eyes of fear?

---

*I don't know what the future holds, Lord, but I
know who holds the future. It's in Your hands,
Father, and I know You have my best interest at
heart. So, instead of letting fear grip my heart,
I choose faith. Instead of worry, I choose joy.
You've proven Your faithfulness time and time
again, Father. I know You won't let me down,
because You never have. Praise You! Amen.*

GOD IS BESIDE YOU

Always remember
That whatever betide you,
You are never alone
For God is beside you.

God is our refuge and strength,
a very present help in trouble.
PSALM 46:1

Has someone betrayed you? How did you feel,
then and now? Have you ever betrayed a friend?

Not everyone can be trusted, Lord. I've learned
this (at times the hard way). But You, Father?
You're not like us humans. You have proven that You
will never let me down, no matter what. You stick
close, even when I go through seasons of trying to
push You away. Have I mentioned how grateful
I am that You don't give up on me, Father? You're
my very best Friend, and I love You. Amen.

HE'S IN CONTROL

Humbly, I realize
That He who made the sea and skies
And holds the whole world in His hand
Also has my small soul in His command.

The law of the LORD is perfect, reviving the
soul. . .the commandment of the LORD
is pure, enlightening the eyes.
PSALM 19:7–8

In what areas do you find it
difficult to give up control?

If You can handle the ocean waves, Father,
You can handle my tumultuous heart. If You can
mold mountains and canyons with Your fingertip,
You can surely mold my will. You are the Creator
of this vast universe. Every living thing bows at
Your name. If You can manage it all with ease,
I know I can trust You with my life, my future,
and my heart. Thank You, Lord. Amen.

Day 276

LET GOD TALK

When your day is pressure-packed
And your hours are all too few,
Just close your eyes and meditate
And let God talk to you.

May my meditation be pleasing to him,
for I rejoice in the LORD.
PSALM 104:34

Are you currently in a stressful time? Can you turn
the situation over to God? If you've already done so,
what measure of peace have you found since?

It's easy to forget, Lord. Sometimes I get so wound
up, so busy, so filled with turmoil, that I forget to
turn to You. I don't share my concerns, my thoughts,
my pains. . . . Today I push the PAUSE button.
I want to take my eyes off the chaos swirling around
me and place them squarely on You, Father.
May I hear Your still, small voice as You whisper
words of peace, love, and guidance. Amen.

STEPPING-STONES

Welcome every stumbling block
And every thorn and jagged rock,
For each one is a stepping-stone
To God who wants you for His own.

He drew me up from the desolate pit,
out of the miry bog, and set my feet upon
a rock, making my steps secure.
PSALM 40:2

How can you show your obedience to God?
Why do people often disobey Him?

It's hard to remember that the things I see as
obstacles are really just stepping-stones, Lord.
I want to avoid them altogether, to wish them
away. But You ask me to speak to each mountain,
to see it as a miracle waiting to happen. You want
to grow me into a mighty woman of God; so today
I choose to face my problems head-on without fear.
Thank You for stepping-stones, Father. Amen.

Day 278

THE POWER OF FAITH

Faith is a force that is greater
Than knowledge or power or skill,
And the darkest defeat turns to triumph
If we trust in God's wisdom and will.

*Trust in the LORD, and do good; so you will dwell in
the land, and enjoy security. . . . Commit your way
to the LORD; trust in him, and he will act.*
PSALM 37:3, 5

When—or why—do you find it difficult
to trust God? Is it easier to trust Him
in the big things or the little things?

---

*Faith is a powerful thing, Lord! It lifts us up above
our circumstances and gives us a completely different
perspective. It causes us to trust as never before and
pushes fear to the depths, where it belongs. I'm so
grateful that I don't have to muster up faith, Father.
You have told me in Your Word that all I need is a
tiny grain of faith, the size of a mustard seed. I think
I can manage that, Lord. Praise You for taking
my faith and using it mightily. Amen.*

GOD'S HELP

Only with the help of God
Can we meet the vast unknown. . .
Even the strongest cannot
Do the job alone!

Be pleased, O God, to deliver me!
O LORD, make haste to help me!
PSALM 70:1

Who in your life is a woman of courage,
like Deborah or Esther? Why did you
choose this particular woman?

I'll admit it, Lord—I often set out on my own
and leave You in the dust. I forget that You're my
Helper, my Friend, my Guide. I want to be the
one pushing my way to the front of the line. Thank
You for the reminder that I can only meet the
vast unknown with Your help. I was never meant
to walk this road alone, nor do I want to. Thank
You for taking me by the hand today, Father,
and thank You for the courage that arises in my
soul when I walk with You. Amen.

Day 280

REJOICE IN ADVERSITY

The way we use adversity
Is strictly our own choice,
For in God's hands adversity
Can make the heart rejoice.

I will rejoice and be glad for thy steadfast love,
because thou hast seen my affliction, thou
hast taken heed of my adversities.
PSALM 31:7

When has your heart rejoiced
during adversity because of God?

I don't always use adversity to my advantage, Lord.
Sometimes I wallow in it, griping and complaining
instead of looking for ways to overcome with joy. I'm
grateful for the freedom to choose, but I recognize the
truth: I must choose to use adversity to my advantage
so that I can grow into a powerful woman of God.
Today I choose to do just that. Thank You for
a new perspective, Father. Amen.

SIMPLE FAITH

Father, grant once more to men
A simple, childlike faith again,
Forgetting color, race, or creed
And seeing only the heart's deep need.

Faith is the assurance of things hoped for,
the conviction of things not seen.
HEBREWS 11:1

Have you totally surrendered your life to Christ?
If not, what is keeping you from doing so?
Do you daily surrender your days to Him?

I'm so moved by the faith of Christians around
the globe, Father. How they inspire me. People
are facing huge challenges—sickness, pain, lack of
water and food—but Your children continue to
walk in faith, no matter what adversity comes
their way. May I learn from the example of these
amazing people, Lord, that I might lean on
You with such amazing faith too. Amen.

Day 282

LET HIM LEAD YOU

Take the Savior's loving hand
And do not try to understand,
Just let Him lead you where He will
Through pastures green, by waters still.

Know that the LORD is God! It is he
that made us, and we are his; we are
his people, and the sheep of his pasture.
PSALM 100:3

How has God ministered to you in a hard place?

_____

I'm a "gotta figure it out" girl, Lord, as You
know. I have a need to know. . .everything.
But, despite my best intentions, there are things
in this life journey that I simply won't understand.
When I face those obstacles, Father, soothe my
troubled mind. Remind me that You know all
and You're taking care of every detail, even the
things that don't make sense to me. I'm so grateful
You have full understanding, Lord. Amen.

A Cup of Kindness

Take a cup of kindness,
Mix it well with love,
Add a lot of patience
And faith in God above.

With patience a ruler may be persuaded,
and a soft tongue will break a bone.
PROVERBS 25:15

If you were to ask God to give you one fruit
of the Spirit, what would it be and why?

I'm grateful for the fruits of the Spirit, Lord—
love, peace, joy, kindness, long-suffering, and so
on. If not for these supernatural "helps" from You,
I wouldn't make it through many of the tough
situations I face. Thank You for the reminder that
You want me to mix up these fruits, Lord, as I deal
with others. Kindness on top of joy on top of peace.
I really can treat others the way I want to be
treated, as long as I do it Your way. Amen.

Day 284

NEW FRIENDS

May we try
In our small way
To make new friends
From day to day.

A faithful envoy brings healing.
PROVERBS 13:17

How can you be a friend today to someone
who needs love or a kind word?

---

*I love my circle of friends, Lord. I'm surrounded by
some amazing people. Today I ask that You grow my
circle. Lead me to new people who can love and be
loved in return. Open my spiritual eyes to see folks in
need of my love and care. Give me wisdom to know
who to approach. Lead me to people who can mentor
and pour into my life, I pray. There are many friends
I haven't met yet, Father, and I'm excited to bump
into them. May it start today. Amen.*

WORDS UNSPOKEN

Prayer is so often just words unspoken,
Whispered in tears by a heart that is broken,
For God is already deeply aware
Of the burdens we find too heavy to bear.

*I am utterly spent and crushed; I groan
because of the tumult of my heart.*
PSALM 38:8

When was the last time you were broken before God,
confessing sin and asking for repentance?
Do you need to do so again?

---

*During seasons of brokenness, I find it hard to
know how to pray, Lord. My heart is so burdened,
so weighted down with tears and pain, that I can
barely utter a word. Thank You for hearing my
heart's cry, even when I'm unable to speak. You get
it. You see beyond my tearful silence. And You care,
Lord. . .deeply. Thank You for being so in tune
with me, Father. I love You so much. Amen.*

STRENGTH AND CHEER

God's kindness is ever around you,
Always ready to freely impart
Strength to your faltering spirit,
Cheer to your lonely heart.

When the cares of my heart are many,
thy consolations cheer my soul.
PSALM 94:19

How can you praise God today for the
works He has done in your life lately?

Your kindness brings strength to my heart, Lord.
I sense it in a coworker's smile, a friend's pat
on the shoulder, a child's giggle. I notice it in
the twinkling eyes of an elderly neighbor, in the
vibrant laughter of a grandchild. You're showering
me with kindness, Father, and I don't want to
miss an opportunity to thank You. Praise You
for Your goodness to me, Lord. Amen.

Day 287

LIFE'S AUTUMN

What a wonderful time is life's autumn,
When the leaves of the trees are all gold,
When God fills each day as He sends it
With memories priceless and old.

One man esteems one day as better than another,
while another man esteems all days alike.
ROMANS 14:5

What memories has God blessed you
with that you prize above others?

I know what it's like to walk through autumn
seasons, Lord. All around me, life seems to be
slowing down. Vibrant summer colors give way to
radiant reds, golds, and oranges. I can sense change
all around me during such seasons, Lord, but I'm not
frightened. I know I can trust You, no matter what
changes come my way. May I enjoy the transition
from one season to the next, Father. Amen.

Day 288

DEEPER BEAUTY

Discipline in daily duty
Will shape your life for deeper beauty,
And as you grow in strength and grace,
The more clearly you can see God's face.

May God be gracious to us and bless us
and make his face to shine upon us.
PSALM 67:1

In what ways do you sometimes
struggle with your daily duties?

Sometimes I need more discipline in my daily
routine, Lord. Things become hum-drum. . .
boring. I procrastinate instead of getting things
done. Thank You for reminding me that there's
beauty, even in the mundane things. When I
lead a disciplined life, I grow in strength and
grace. Help me today, I pray. Amen.

GOD IS REAL

What better answers are there
To prove God's holy being
Than the wonders all around us
That are ours just for the seeing.

"Stop and consider the wondrous works of God."
JOB 37:14

What things in nature give you great joy?
A tiny hummingbird, a majestic mountain,
the changing of the seasons, the wind on
your face, the beauty of pristine snow?

---

*I often wonder how people can claim You
don't exist, Father. Don't they see You in every
mountain peak? Can't they sense Your presence
in the dew the morning grass? Aren't they aware
of Your symphony in a bird's song? You are truly
magnificent, God, and all of nature agrees.
Today, may people around the globe awaken to
the majestic song Your creation sings. Amen.*

Day 290

WALK WITH HIM

May you walk with Him
And dwell in His love
As He sends you good gifts
From heaven above.

*Walk in love, as Christ loved us
and gave himself up for us.*
EPHESIANS 5:2

What is the difference between
a "want" and a "need"?

---

*I find it hard to differentiate between wants
and needs sometimes, Lord. I want something so
badly that it actually feels like a legitimate need.
I ask You to shine Your light on these things I feel
so strongly about, Father. Give me clarity to tell
the difference between a bona fide need and a
simple desire or want. May I long solely for
the things that please Your heart. Amen.*

Day 291

REAL CONTENTMENT

It's by completing
What God gives us to do
That we find real contentment
And happiness, too.

Requite them according to their work, and according to
the evil of their deeds; requite them according to the
work of their hands; render them their due reward.
PSALM 28:4

What jobs do you find satisfaction in doing?

There's great satisfaction in working for You,
Lord. And nothing feels better than completing a
God-ordained task. Thank You for entrusting me
with kingdom work. I'm so grateful to offer my
gifts, my talents, my time. . . . May I never become
discontent with working for You, Father. Amen.

THE IMPORTANCE OF PRAYER

Whenever you are hurried
And must leave something undone,
Be sure it's not your prayer to God
At dawn or setting sun.

*It is good to give thanks to the LORD, to sing praises
to thy name, O Most High; to declare thy steadfast
love in the morning, and thy faithfulness by night.*
PSALM 92:1–2

Imagine yourself at God's feet.
What is He saying to you?

---

*I lead such a busy life, Lord. Sometimes I neglect
my quiet time with You. I step into my day
without asking for Your guidance, Your blessing,
Your wisdom. I drop off to sleep at night without
thanking You for the many times You provided for
me throughout the day. Please forgive me, Father,
and help me to keep You in the top spot. You are
worthy of my praise, Lord—morning,
noon, and night. Amen.*

Day 293

A Cheerful Song

I sometimes think that friendliness
Is something like a cheerful song. . .
It makes the good days better,
And it helps when things go wrong.

*The LORD is my strength and my shield; in him
my heart trusts; so I am helped, and my heart
exults, and with my song I give thanks to him.*
PSALM 28:7

What have you learned from a friend this week?

---

*Have I taken the time to thank You for my friends
lately, Lord? They bring comfort on pain-filled days,
joy when I'm down in the dumps, and wisdom when
I don't know which way to turn. They make every
day better, and I'm so very grateful for them, Father.
Thank You for each and every one, Lord. Amen.*

Day 294

Nighttime Prayers

I meet God in the morning
And go with Him through the day,
Then in the stillness of the night
Before sleep comes, I pray.

*I rise before dawn and cry for help; I hope in thy
words. My eyes are awake before the watches of
the night, that I may meditate upon thy promise.*
Psalm 119:147–148

Are you guilty of neglecting your prayer life?
How can you change that this week?

---

*Each morning is filled with hope, Lord. I see Your
hand at work, even before I lift my head from the
pillow. I praise You for the day ahead, because I
know it will be filled with endless possibilities.
My heart continues to reach out to You as the
hours tick by. And when I crawl back into bed
at night, I'm keenly aware of Your presence.
What an amazing Father You are! Amen.*

Day 295

A New Day

See the dew glisten as a new day is born,
Hear the birds sing on the wings
of the morn.

From the rising of the sun to its setting
the name of the LORD is to be praised!
PSALM 113:3

Do you like to hear the birds sing? What are your
thoughts when you hear them in the morning?

There's something so magical about the
morning, Father! Reminders of Your presence
are everywhere—in the dewy grass, in the
bird's song, and in the clear blue sky above.
Hope reigns in the morning and offers a world
of possibilities. Thank You for giving Your creation
a fresh new start every day, Lord. My heart is
renewed with each morning's dawn. Amen.

THE TEMPLE OF GOD

The house of prayer is no farther away
Than the quiet spot where you kneel and pray,
For the heart is a temple when God is there
As you place yourself in His loving care.

I bow down toward thy holy temple and
give thanks to thy name for thy steadfast love
and thy faithfulness; for thou hast exalted
above everything thy name and thy word.
PSALM 138:2

Do you have special places or times
of day when you like to talk with God?

I'm not looking for a majestic cathedral or
stained-glass windows, Father. I don't need a
place of opulence to meet with You. I can cry out
to You wherever I happen to be at any given
moment—on the subway, in a public restaurant,
walking into my workplace. You're ever present,
Father, and ready to hear from me, any time,
any place. It's refreshing to know that I can cry
out to You, even now. Praise You, Father! Amen.

Keep Climbing

Faith is a mover of mountains,
And there's nothing that God cannot do,
So start out today with faith in your heart
And climb till your dream comes true!

*Lord, thou hast been our dwelling place in all
generations. Before the mountains were brought forth,
or ever thou hadst formed the earth and the world,
from everlasting to everlasting thou art God.*
Psalm 90:1–2

What are you believing by faith
that the Lord will do for you?

---

*I've faced many mountains in my life, Lord.
And they presented a challenge. In fact, many
stopped me in my tracks. I'm so grateful for the
promise in Your Word that mountains are nothing
to You. You've given me the supernatural power to
speak to them—in Your name—and watch them be
cast into the sea. Today I speak to the mountains in
front of me. Be gone, in Jesus' name! Amen.*

Day 298

A FORTRESS OF FAITH

Be not disheartened by troubles,
For trials are the building blocks
On which to erect a fortress of faith
Secure on God's ageless rocks.

In thee, O Lord, do I take refuge; let me never be put
to shame! . . . Be thou to me a rock of refuge, a strong
fortress, to save me, for thou art my rock and my fortress.
PSALM 71:1, 3

What Bible verse can you set in
your heart as a shield against fear?

If trials are spiritual building blocks, then I've
got a mountain of them, Lord! I've certainly
faced many trials in my life over the years.
When I look back, I see a fortress of faith, which
helped me through every challenge. Thank You for
being my refuge during troubled times, Lord.
What a wonderful shield You are! Amen.

Day 299

THE BLESSINGS OF FRIENDSHIP

Father, make us kind and wise
So we may always recognize
The blessings that are ours to take
And the friendships that are ours to make.

*There are friends who pretend to be friends, but
there is a friend who sticks closer than a brother.*
PROVERBS 18:24

How can you grow in wisdom?

---

*I learn so much from my friends, Lord. They are
among life's best teachers. From them, I've learned
how to overcome obstacles, forgive those who hurt
me, and face life's challenges with a smile. Thank You
for entrusting these wonderful people to me, Lord.
I cherish each one as a gift, straight from You.
Praise You for friendship, Father. Amen.*

Day 300

A HAPPY HEART

Cheerful thoughts like sunbeams
Lighten up the darkest fears,
For when the heart is happy
There's just no time for tears.

A glad heart makes a cheerful countenance,
but by sorrow of heart the spirit is broken.
PROVERBS 15:13

Do you have a grateful spirit—toward your job,
your family, your home, and others?

I love the image of cheerful thoughts being like
sunbeams, Lord. They truly can burst through the
clouds and bring hope where once there was none.
May I be one who spreads cheer everywhere I go,
Lord. I want to radiate joy and hopefulness to all
I meet along life's path. May others know, by my
cheerful countenance, that life in You is filled
with amazing possibilities. Amen.

Day 301

WALK HUMBLY

Do justice, love kindness,
walk humbly with God. . .
All things worth having
are yours to achieve
If you follow God's words
and have faith to believe!

*He loves righteousness and justice; the earth
is full of the steadfast love of the LORD.*
PSALM 33:5

Can you list ten of your good qualities and five
of your weaknesses? Read aloud the list of your good
qualities, and give God your weaknesses.

---

*What a wonderful mandate, Lord! I long to do
all of those things—to walk humbly with You,
not puffed up and arrogant. To do justice to all I
come in contact with—those who think like me
and those I disagree with. To love kindness—to the
point where it's second nature to spread kindness
to all I meet along life's path. Thank You for
guiding me through Your Word, Father. Amen.*

Day 302

THE NEEDED SPARK

An unlit candle gives no light—
Only when burning is it shining bright;
And if life is empty, dull, and dark,
It's doing things for others
that gives the needed spark.

Yea, thou dost light my lamp; the LORD
my God lightens my darkness.
PSALM 18:28

How can you bless your minister or
your minister's spouse this week?

I want to be effective for You, Lord—not a candle
that refuses to be lit, but one that shines brightly
so that others will be drawn to You. What would
be the point of living my life, dull and dark,
refusing to shine? May I be known as one who
takes full advantage of her faith, ready to
share Your love to all I meet. Amen.

BITTER AND SWEET

Everything is by comparison
Both the bitter and the sweet,
And it takes a bit of both of them
To make our lives complete.

*He who is sated loathes honey, but to one
who is hungry everything bitter is sweet.*
PROVERBS 27:7

What things in your life are "bitter"? What things are
"sweet"? How can you learn to appreciate both?

---

*I've often found it hard to accept the bitter
things in life, Lord. I want everything to be
sweet. But I can see that it would be impossible
to enjoy the sweet if I didn't have the contrast
of the bitter. The hard times are growing me
into a stronger woman, Father, and I need that.
May I learn from both the good and the bad
that come my way, Lord. Amen.*

Day 304

LOVING HEARTS

Some folks grow older
with birthdays, it's true,
But others grow nicer
as years widen their view.
No one will notice a few little wrinkles
When a kind, loving heart fills
the eyes full of twinkles.

Grandchildren are the crown of the aged.
PROVERBS 17:6

How do you feel you are aging?
Are you growing nicer as the years go by?

---

*I don't mind aging, Lord, as long as I can do it with
my hand in Yours. In many ways I'm beginning to
understand the phrase "We don't get older; we get
better." For certain, I feel wiser and closer to You
than ever before. So, Lord, let the birthdays come.
Let the calendar do its work. I'll stick with You for
the rest of this amazing journey, Father. Amen.*

Day 305

THE MASTER PLAN

All things work together
To complete the master plan,
And God up in heaven
Can see what's best for man.

*Yet God my King is from of old, working
salvation in the midst of the earth.*
PSALM 74:12

What do you do when a
cherished dream falls apart?

---

*Father, when things begin to fall apart, may I
not panic! Remind me, even in the very middle
of the unraveling, that You have an awesome
"plan and will bring it to fruition despite any
bumps in the road. All things really do work
together for good, Lord. May I never ever forget
that biblical promise. Thank You! Amen.*

EVERYTHING IS HIS

Someday may man realize
That all the earth, the seas, and skies
Belong to God, who made us all,
The rich, the poor, the great, the small.

Who has ascended to heaven and come down?
Who has gathered the wind in his fists? Who has
wrapped up the waters in a garment? Who has
established all the ends of the earth? What is his
name, and what is his son's name? Surely you know!
PROVERBS 30:4

How do you acquire inspiration? Think about
a time that you were overwhelmed by God's
greatness. What effect did that have on you?

It all belongs to You, Lord—the earth, the seas,
the sky, the stars, and everything beyond what
we can see with human eyes. You're the Author of
all of it. May we never forget that You see across
this great planet and care deeply about all of its
inhabitants. We all belong to You, our great
and loving Father. Bless You! Amen.

PATIENCE AND GRACE

God, give us patience and grace to endure
And a stronger faith so we feel secure
And instead of remembering,
help us forget
The irritations that caused us to fret.

*Therefore, as God's chosen people, holy and dearly
loved, clothe yourselves with compassion,
kindness, humility, gentleness and patience.*
COLOSSIANS 3:12 NIV

Do you catch yourself complaining or find
yourself easily irritated? How can you work on
these attitudes to show a more Christlike one?

---

*I'll admit it, Lord: fretting has been my natural
response to life's challenges. I've allowed it to rise
to the surface many times. Today, instead of fretting,
I choose to let go of the irritations that plague me.
I won't rehearse them in my mind. I won't let
them eat me up. Instead, I choose compassion,
kindness, humility, gentleness, and patience.
I need Your help, Father! Amen.*

GROW IN THE HARD TIMES

Trouble is part and parcel of life,
And no man can grow without
trouble and strife,
And the steep hills ahead and
the high mountain peaks
Afford man at last the peace that he seeks.

"You will go out in joy and be led forth in peace;
the mountains and hills will burst into song before you,
and all the trees of the field will clap their hands."
ISAIAH 55:12 NIV

Has peace come at a high cost to you?
Are you still looking for peace? How is God
helping you through these challenges?

It would be wonderful to live a pain-free life,
Lord. How awesome, to have no troubles at all!
Still, I've come to understand that You are leading
me, not from trouble to trouble, but from joy to joy.
Each struggle I face is growing me into a mighty
woman of God, one who understands the true
meaning of peace. Thank You for helping me
through life's challenges, Father. Amen.

Day 309

KINDNESS MATTERS

A warm, ready smile or a kind,
thoughtful deed
Or a hand outstretched
in an hour of need
Can change our outlook
and make the world bright
Where a minute before just
nothing seemed right.

*A brother helped is like a strong city,
but quarreling is like the bars of a castle.*
PROVERBS 18:19

When has a smile meant a great deal to you? When
have you helped someone by offering a smile?

*Father, thank You for surrounding me with
people who offer a smile or a cheerful "Hello."
They brighten my days and bring hope during
hard seasons. May I be that sort of friend to
others, Lord. I want to radiate Your love and
Your joy to people who are hurting. Help me
to be a shining reflection of You. Amen.*

Day 310

KINDRED HEARTS

The golden chain of friendship
Is a strong and blessed tie
Binding kindred hearts together
As the years go passing by.

*Do good, O LORD, to those who are good,
and to those who are upright in their hearts!*
PSALM 125:4

What fond remembrances do you have of
times with friends or family? What are
those links that bound you together in love?

---

*Friends have made this life extra special, Father.
Thank You for each one. Today I'm especially
grateful for those who've stood the test of time—
the ones who know me best and love me anyway.
I cherish the chain of friendship with these people,
especially, because we are bound together by time
and circumstance. May we have many more
blessed years together. Amen!*

A GENTLE HEART

God in His loving and all-wise way
Makes the heart that was young one day
Serene and more gentle
and less restless, too,
Content to remember the
joys it once knew.

Remember, LORD, your great mercy
and love, for they are from of old.
PSALM 25:6 NIV

Why does God say women who have a gentle and
quiet spirit are of great worth to God (1 Peter 3:3–5)?
How do you rank, on a scale of 1 to 10?

There have been seasons when I've felt restless, Lord.
Discontentment reigned. I would have settled into
this routine, if not for You. Father, You spoke to me
in that soothing voice of Yours and calmed my heart.
You brought contentment instead of restlessness. You
ignited my spirit, and joy entered my life once more.
How can I ever thank You? I'm so blessed. Amen.

Day 312

HEARTFELT CONVERSATION

Take ample time
For heartfelt conversation,
Establish with our Father
An unbreakable relation.

*A word fitly spoken is like apples of gold
in a setting of silver.*
PROVERBS 25:11

We are told to "pray constantly" (1 Thessalonians
5:17). Do you find this instruction to be a
challenge? Are you striving toward this goal?

---

*Lord, it's so good to talk with You. I love the idea that
I don't have to be in a special place at a special time. I
can talk with You anywhere. Today, I specifically ask
that You slow me down so that I take adequate time
to share everything on my heart and listen for Your
response. I know there are things You're longing to tell
me too, Lord. My ears are wide open today, Father.
Thanks for caring. . .and sharing. Amen.*

Day 313

A PERFECT PLAN

God does nothing without purpose—
Everything's a perfect plan
To fulfill in bounteous measure
All He has ever promised man.

Cast your cares on the LORD and he will sustain you.
PSALM 55:22 NIV

What promises has God already
fulfilled for you or in you?

---

*It's taken me awhile to realize that You have
a plan and a purpose for my life, Father.
Sometimes I set out with specific goals and
don't meet them. . .then give up. You're not like
that. If You said it, You will bring it to pass.
And while I may not always understand what
You're up to, I know I can trust You, Father.
You're fulfilling a much higher purpose in me,
even now. I praise You, Lord. Amen.*

GIFTS ALL AROUND

Every happy happening
And every lucky break
Are little gifts from God above
That are ours to freely take.

The steps of a man are from the LORD, *and he*
establishes him in whose way he delights.
PSALM 37:23

Has God provided for all your needs?
Has He provided for some of your wants?

I know there's no such thing as good luck, Lord.
Each blessing comes straight from Your hand,
a gift from above. Nothing is by chance. I'm so
grateful for the way You provide for me, Father.
You make sure I have all I need and more. What a
generous heavenly Father You are. Praise You! Amen.

Day 315

THE HEART'S HAVEN

Help all people everywhere
who must often dwell apart
To know that they're together
in the haven of the heart.

If we love one another, God abides
in us and his love is perfected in us.
1 JOHN 4:12

What unused or unnecessary things in
your home can you give away to others?

Living in community is a wonderful thing,
Father. It's too hard to try to make it on our
own. Thank You for surrounding us with folks
who can "do life" with us. We were never meant
to fight solo through life's battles. Your love is
perfected in us when we choose to love one
another. What a terrific way to live. Amen.

Day 316

NO MORE CARES

I pray that God will just take over
All the problems I couldn't solve,
And I'm ready for tomorrow
With all my cares dissolved.

*Even the sparrow finds a home, and the swallow
a nest for herself, where she may lay her young,
at thy altars, O LORD of hosts, my King and my God.*
PSALM 84:3

List two things you worry about the most.
How can you overcome a habit of worry and
place your trust in God for these things?

---

*I would like to think that I can fix anything,
Lord, that no problem is too big for me. But
You and I both know that's not true. My cares
are never truly dissolved until I place them at
Your feet. Even then I fight to let go. Today
I choose to let go of worry by releasing my
grip on the problems I've clung so tightly to.
They are no longer mine, Father. I place
them at the foot of Your throne. Amen.*

GROWING OLDER

Growing older only means
The spirit grows serene,
And we behold things with our souls
That our eyes have never seen.

Even to old age and gray hairs, O God,
do not forsake me, till I proclaim thy
might to all the generations to come.
PSALM 71:18

How do the examples of biblical men
and women inspire and encourage you?

I hope I live to be a ripe old age, Lord. There are
so many roads still untraveled in my journey,
after all. As I age, please give me wisdom and peace.
Help me to see things with an eternal perspective.
I will follow You, Father, all the days of my life,
no matter how long that might be. Amen.

Day 318

THE VIRTUE OF KINDNESS

Kindness is a virtue
Given by the Lord,
It pays dividends in happiness
And joy is its reward.

*A wicked man earns deceptive wages, but one
who sows righteousness gets a sure reward.*
PROVERBS 11:18

When has doing something for others
made you happy? What have you
done for those less fortunate?

---

*You've been so good and kind to me, Lord. I haven't
always deserved it, but that didn't stop You! People
in my world don't always deserve kindness from me
either; but still I want to follow in Your footsteps
and offer it. The payoff will be great. In fact, there
will be a boomerang effect. I will be treated kindly
by others if I reach out to them in a loving fashion.
Thank You for this reminder. Amen.*

A Thankful Heart

The joy of enjoying
And the fullness of living
Are found in the heart
That is filled with thanksgiving.

Deceit is in the heart of those who devise
evil, but those who plan good have joy.
Proverbs 12:20

How can you cultivate an
atmosphere of joy in your home?

My heart is so full, Father! You've given me joy
that bubbles over and spills out onto everyone
I meet. Thank You for filling my soul with
thanksgiving, even during the tough seasons.
May joy always lead the way, Lord, splashing
over onto friends and strangers alike. Amen.

Day 320

WONDERFUL WORLD

It's a wonderful world and it always will be
If we keep our eyes open and focused to see
The wonderful things man is capable of
When he opens his heart to
God and His love.

*God looks down from heaven upon the sons of men to see
if there are any that are wise, that seek after God.*
PSALM 53:2

Where do you see God best reflected in humankind?
How can you encourage others to continue to
do the "wonderful things" they are capable of,
instead of giving in to a sinful nature?

*Thank You for the reminder, Lord, that people are
good! This big, wide world is filled with folks who
are capable of so much goodness. May You open the
hearts of all mankind to know You, love You, and
receive You, that all might join You in heaven one
day. Until then, thank You for surrounding me
with wonderfully amazing people. Amen.*

Day 321

CREATIVE GOD

In the beauty of a snowflake,
Falling softly on the land,
Is the mystery and miracle
Of God's great, creative hand!

Praise the LORD from the earth, you. . .fire and hail,
snow and frost, stormy wind fulfilling his command!
PSALM 148:7–8

How is the world better because we are
as individual as the snowflakes?

Father, thank You for reminding me that we
are all unique and beautiful in Your sight.
We are as individual as the snowflakes, each
different but created by You. How boring this
world would be if we were all alike, Lord.
Thanks for making me unique. I'm so grateful to
be exactly who You've created me to be. Amen.

Day 322

ALL GOD ASKS

It's hard to believe
That God asks no more
Than to bring Him our problems
And then close the door.

The LORD is a stronghold for the oppressed,
a stronghold in times of trouble. And those who
know thy name put their trust in thee, for thou,
O LORD, hast not forsaken those who seek thee.
PSALM 9:9–10

What issues in your life are you
currently having difficulty letting go of?

You've asked me to bring my problems to You and
then let go, God. I'll admit that I don't always do
that. I come to You, ready to release my concerns,
but sometimes I sweep them back into my arms once
again. I needed the reminder that releasing things
to You is a forever choice, Lord. No more back-and-
forth movement from me. I trust You, Father. Amen.

MY PRAYER FOR TODAY

I give to You my thanks
And my heart kneels to pray—
God keep me and guide me
And go with me today.

Thou dost guide me with thy counsel,
and afterward thou wilt receive me to glory.
PSALM 73:24

How have you seen God guide
you in your everyday life?

You're the best Guide ever, Lord. You created
all things, so You're keenly aware of what's on
the path in front of me. There are times when
I'm unsure of my next step, but You stand ready,
hand extended, to lead the way down the path
toward the future. I'm so excited about where
You're taking me, Lord! Amen.

Day 324

THE KEY TO LIVING

Help us to remember
That the key to life and living
Is to make each prayer a prayer of thanks
And every day "Thanksgiving."

I will praise the name of God with a song;
I will magnify him with thanksgiving.
PSALM 69:30

What talents or gifts did God instill in you?
How are you using these gifts to help others?

Thank You for the gifts You've placed inside of me,
Lord. I want to learn how to use them all for You,
so that I can touch this world on a day-to-day
basis. Every day can truly be Thanksgiving when I
remember that these precious gifts are meant just for
me. How kind You are to me, Father! Amen.

Day 325

REAL THANKSGIVING

Dear God, no words are great enough
to thank You for just living,
And that is why every day is
a day for real thanksgiving.

Let us come into his presence with thanksgiving;
let us make a joyful noise to him with songs of praise!
PSALM 95:2

Have you thanked God today for the lives
of your family and those who are close to you?

This is a new day, Lord. You've given me
breath in my lungs, joy for the journey, and
strength to face any challenges ahead. This day
is like a gift to me, Father. May I never forget
that each precious moment with You is a present.
Today I choose to celebrate each moment and do
my best to make each one count. Amen.

Day 326

UNCOUNTED JEWELS

God's heavens are dotted
with uncounted jewels,
For joy without measure
is one of God's rules,
His hand is so generous,
His heart is so great,
He comes not too soon,
and He comes not too late.

*Of old thou didst lay the foundation of the earth,
and the heavens are the work of thy hands.*
PSALM 102:25

Reflect on a time when you felt you were waiting on
the Lord. How did He come through for you—
even if His timing was different than yours?

*I'm glad You're a "just in time" God. You don't
show up early. You're never late. You're always
right on time. The next time I doubt You, when
I wonder if You're going to come through for
me, remind me that You haven't failed me yet.
If You laid the foundations of the world,
surely You can look after my needs. Amen.*

Day 327

ENDLESS SUPPLY

God, I know that I love You,
And I know without doubt
That Your goodness and mercy
Never run out.

Have mercy on me, O God, according to thy
steadfast love; according to thy abundant
mercy blot out my transgressions.
PSALM 51:1

How can you extend God's goodness
and mercy to others this week?

I'm always running out of things, Lord—groceries,
money, time, and so many other things besides.
My provisions might run low at times, but Yours
never do. You have a vast, abundant supply. . .
of everything. Your well will never run dry.
And, as Your child, You'll make sure I have all
I need as well. Praise You, Lord! Amen.

THE EARTH IS HIS

"The earth is the Lord's
And the fullness thereof"—
It speaks of His greatness,
It sings of His love.

The heavens are thine, the earth also is thine; the
world and all that is in it, thou hast founded them.
PSALM 89:11

How would you describe the Lord Almighty?

I take ownership of so many things, Lord—
my home, my car, my possessions. Yet, I know in
reality that none of it actually belongs to me.
I can't take it with me when I go. You, on the other
hand? You own everything! The stars, the earth,
the sky, the seas, the mountains, the valleys, and
everything in between. All belong to You, and all
are loved by You. Praise You, Father! Amen.

STOP AND PRAY

Do you pause in meditation
Upon life's thoroughfare,
And offer up thanksgiving—
Or say a word of prayer?

I revere thy commandments, which I love,
and I will meditate on thy statutes.
PSALM 119:48

How do you consciously take the time to be still in
your daily schedule? Is there anything you need
to cut out to allow for more time in meditation?

Life is, indeed, a thoroughfare, Lord. At least, that's
the way it feels at times. I find myself on a proverbial
racetrack, buzzing along toward this goal or that
goal, all the while losing sight of You. Today I make
a conscious effort to slow down, to spend more time
in meditation and communion with You. It feels
good to hit the PAUSE *button, Lord. Amen.*

Day 330

SWEET FORBEARANCE

Teach me sweet forbearance
When things do not go right,
So I remain unruffled
When others grow uptight.

*If you faint in the day of adversity,
your strength is small.*
PROVERBS 24:10

What Bible verse can you set in your
heart when you need patience?

---

*Forbearance is not my strong suit, Lord, as You
well know! I'm not always the most patient,
trusting person, especially when things seem to be
going against me. Today I choose to be unruffled,
unscathed. My days of giving up are behind me.
From now on, I'll do my best to keep on keeping
on, no matter what comes my way. Amen.*

JOY EVERY STEP

Prayers are the stairs that lead to God,
And there's joy every step of the way
When we make our pilgrimage to Him
With love in our hearts each day.

The steps of a man are from the LORD, and he
establishes him in whose way he delights.
PSALM 37:23

Do you need to take time to
rest and recharge today?

Every prayer is a step toward You, Lord. And
though it's not always easy, I'm happy to make the
climb. In fact, I'm learning to look for joy in the
journey, even on the days when climbing is steep.
I'll keep my focus on You, Father, and You will
direct my path. I'm so grateful. Amen.

A QUIET HEART

Teach me how to quiet
My racing, rising heart
So I may hear the answer
You are trying to impart.

My son, give me your heart,
and let your eyes observe my ways.
PROVERBS 23:26

Do you ever assume what God's answers are
going to be to your petitions without really
taking the time to listen? What happens
when your assumptions are incorrect?

Making assumptions comes naturally to me, Lord,
but You ask me not to do that, especially where
You're concerned. I have to lay down preconceived
ideas and trust You. Today I choose to sit quietly
and listen to Your still, small voice. You will tell me
what I need to know. I won't need to assume any
longer because I will hear Your voice. Thanks for
speaking to me, Father. Amen.

Day 333

GIVE AND GIVE AND GIVE AGAIN

Only what we give away
Enriches us from day to day.

He who sows sparingly will also reap sparingly, and he
who sows bountifully will also reap bountifully.
2 CORINTHIANS 9:6

When have you given more than you
thought you could? What kind of
blessings did you experience in return?

Above and beyond, Lord. That's how You
challenge me to live, and that's how You challenge
me to give. Only through abundant giving will
I ever experience abundant living. So, today I
choose to dig deep and give more—of my time,
talents, and treasures. I know that my life will be
enriched as a result of what I'm willing to let
go of. What a remarkable concept! Amen.

Day 334

HE UNDERSTANDS

Whenever you are troubled,
Put your problems in God's hand,
For He has faced all problems,
And He will understand.

*"Glory to God in the highest heaven, and on
earth peace to those on whom his favor rests."*
LUKE 2:14 NIV

Do you ever doubt the Lord's love for you?
How has God spoken the truth to you in the
past to help you overcome these doubts?

---

*It's remarkable to think that You don't just see
my troubles, Lord. . .You understand them. You
empathize. It truly wows me to realize that the
Creator of all knows and fully understands what
I'm up against. Because I know You understand
what I'm going through, I can trust You with every
detail. And today I choose to do just that. Amen.*

Day 335

GOD'S LOVING CARE

Place yourself in God's loving care,
And He will gladly help you bear
Whatever lies ahead of you,
And He will see you safely through.

"Behold, God is my salvation; I will trust, and will
not be afraid; for the LORD GOD is my strength
and my song, and he has become my salvation."
ISAIAH 12:2

What times of challenge or rejoicing are forthcoming
in your life? Ask God to prepare you for each.

I love the idea that You are bearing my burdens,
Lord. It's almost as if You're physically lifting
me above the circumstances. In order for that to
happen, I have to submit to Your will and Your
plan. I've got to place myself in Your care so that
You can take it from there. Today I choose to give
my burdens to You. I'm Yours, Father! Amen.

Day 336

THE BEST OF DAYS

With a sweet nostalgia we longingly recall
The happy days of long ago
that seem the best of all.

I have been young, and now am old.
PSALM 37:25

What are some of your favorite holiday memories
you've made with your family? What new traditions
can you incorporate to make new memories?

---

*I've been blessed with some lovely memories,
Father. So many happy times to look back on. Thank
You for filling my past with joy, my present with
hopefulness, and my future with possibilities. Every
day with You is my very best day, Lord. Amen.*

MY COMFORTER

Oh, God, what a comfort
To know that You care
And to know when I seek You,
You will always be there!

"As for me, I would seek God, and to
God would I commit my cause."
JOB 5:8

Why is mercy important? When in
your life have you been shown mercy?

Finding people who genuinely care about what I'm
going through isn't always easy, Lord. That's why
I'm so glad I have You. I don't have to plead my
case with You or hope that You empathize. You care.
Sincerely. This brings me such comfort, Father. You're
always there for me, and I'm so grateful. Amen.

Day 338

HIS HOLY BIRTH

The holy Christ Child came
down to live on earth,
And that is why we celebrate
His holy, wondrous birth.

*"For to you is born this day in the city of
David a Savior, who is Christ the Lord."*
LUKE 2:11

Which biblical story means the most to you?
What Bible character can you relate to the most?

---

*Father, I'm so grateful that You sent Your Son
from heaven to earth. I can't even imagine the
sorrow it must have caused to ask Him to leave the
portals of heaven and venture to that little stable
in Bethlehem, but I know the impact His coming
had on my life. How can I ever thank You for such
an amazing gift? What a Savior! Amen.*

GOD'S DIVINE GIFT

What is love? No words can define it.
It's something so great,
only God could design it.
Yes, love is beyond what man can define,
For love is immortal and
God's gift divine.

To him who alone does great wonders,
for his steadfast love endures for ever.
PSALM 136:4

What is the best gift you've ever received?
What is the best gift you've ever given?

The gift of Your Son was, by far, the greatest
present I've ever received. Though I've opened
many presents and packages over the years, nothing
will even come close to the finest gift of all. Best of
all, You freely offer the gift of Your Son to all who
would draw near to Him and call on His name.
What a generous God You are! Amen.

Day 340

OPEN THE DOOR

We open the door to let joy walk through
When we learn to expect
the best and most, too,
For believing we'll find a happy surprise
Makes reality out of a fancied surmise!

*May the God of hope fill you with all joy
and peace in believing, so that by the power
of the Holy Spirit you may abound in hope.*
ROMANS 15:13

What has been your happiest
surprise in your life so far?

---

*I'm hoping for the best, Lord. My perspective has
shifted to one of positivity, thanks to You. You've
got surprises ahead for me, a road paved with
possibilities. I'm sure of it. Until I see what
You have in store for me with my own eyes, I'm
remaining in a hopeful, positive stance. You delight
me at every turn, Father, and I'm grateful! Amen.*

Day 341

A LOVING HEART

Remember, a kind and thoughtful deed
Or a hand outstretched in time of need
Is the rarest of gifts, for it is a part
Not of the purse, but a loving heart.

Little children, let us not love in word
or speech but in deed and in truth.
1 JOHN 3:18

What intangible gifts have meant
the most to you and why?

I love gifts from the heart, Father—a sweet
card from a friend, a kind word from my boss,
a thank-you note, an unexpected lunch date
with a loved one I haven't seen in a while.
All of these serve as reminders of Your goodness
and Your presence. They're better than any
tangible gift I might receive, Father. Thank
You for these little surprises. Amen.

Day 342

GOD'S FACE

The silent stars in timeless skies,
The wonderment in children's eyes,
A rosebud in a slender vase
Are all reflections of God's face.

*Hear, O LORD, when I cry aloud, be gracious to
me and answer me! Thou hast said, "Seek ye my
face." My heart says to thee, "Thy face, LORD,
do I seek." Hide not thy face from me.*
PSALM 27:7–9

What have you learned about God
and the world through children?

---

*It's almost as if I'm looking into Your eyes each time
I see stars twinkling in the sky above, Lord. And
when I look at children—the innocence in each tiny
face—I envision Your love pouring out for me.
You're everywhere, Father—always reminding me
of Your great love for me. I'm so thankful. Amen.*

Day 343

PEACE AND GOODWILL

We pray to Thee, our Father,
As Christmas comes again,
For peace among all nations
And goodwill between all men.

"Whatever house you enter, first say,
'Peace be to this house!'"
LUKE 10:5

Though it may not be on an international scale,
how can you promote goodwill where you are?

Let there be peace on earth, Lord. I say it all the
time. We even sing it. But I often wonder if
it will ever truly come to pass. There's so much
turmoil across this vast planet. I know, based on
Your Word, there's coming a day when every knee
will bow and every tongue proclaim that You are
God. Only then will we ever truly see peace, Lord.
And until then, I will continue to pray. Amen.

Day 344

ONLY JESUS

Only through the Christ Child
can man be born again,
For God sent the baby Jesus
as the Savior of all men.

*This is how the birth of Jesus the Messiah came
about: His mother Mary was pledged to be married
to Joseph, but before they came together, she was
found to be pregnant through the Holy Spirit.*
MATTHEW 1:18 NIV

When you picture Jesus as a tiny baby,
what are your feelings and thoughts?

---

*Father, I've often wondered why You chose
Mary to bring Your Son into the world. Just
a simple, humble girl. Were You pleased with
her heart? Warmed by her kindness to others?
Touched by how she treated the children in her
circle? I may never know, Lord, but I'm so
glad You handpicked her to carry baby Jesus,
both in her womb and her arms. I praise
You for trusting her for such a task. Amen.*

No Reason at All

In counting our blessings,
We find when we're through
We've no reason at all
To complain or be blue.

A faithful man will abound with blessings.
PROVERBS 28:20

For what reason, characteristic, personality trait,
or act of kindness do you wish to be remembered?

---

*I've counted my many blessings, Father, and
have been reminded of Your overwhelming
goodness to me! You sent Your only Son as a babe
in a manger, knowing He would one day die on
a cross. . .for sinners like me. You poured out love,
healing, and so much more, Lord. During the
Christmas season I'm particularly touched by
the gift of Your Son. Praise You! Amen.*

Day 346

THE FIRST CHRISTMAS

May the holy remembrance
Of the first Christmas Day
Be our reassurance
Christ is not far away.

Upon thee was I cast from my birth, and since
my mother bore me thou hast been my God.
PSALM 22:10

What can you do to brighten your
coworker's or neighbor's day?

Emmanuel. God with us. Father, You knew in
advance that it would come to this—that we would
sin and fall short of Your goodness. That we would
need a Savior, One willing to give His very life for
a broken, dying world. During the Christmas season
I'm completely overwhelmed by such a remarkable
gift. Thank You for coming close, Emmanuel. You
truly are with us—now and forever. Amen.

Day 347

GOOD CHEER

May every heart and every home
Continue through the year
To feel the warmth and wonderment
Of this season of good cheer.

The unfolding of thy words gives light;
it imparts understanding to the simple.
PSALM 119:130

What is your favorite Christmas tradition?
Why is it special to you?

I just love the Christmas season, Lord!
It warms the heart and pulls people together.
Listening to Christmas carols playing inside of
stores makes me so happy. Watching parents
shop for gifts for their little ones brings joy too.
Even the chaos of last-minute purchases can be
fun, for giving is truly the spirit of the season.
What a wonderful time of year, Lord. Amen.

Day 348

ETERNAL GLORY

Make us aware
That the Christmas story
Is everyone's promise
Of eternal glory.

*Not to us, O LORD, not to us, but to thy
name give glory, for the sake of thy
steadfast love and thy faithfulness!*
PSALM 115:1

What can you do to give love away today—
without buying, boxing, wrapping, or tying?
How can you show that God is love?

---

*Without Christmas, Lord, where would we
be? People across this great big world would
be without hope, lost in sin. When You came
up with the plan to send Jesus, it changed
everything. You made a way out for us, Father.
That amazing promise gives every believer eternal
life. What a story, Lord! Best gift ever! Amen.*

Day 349

A BETTER PLACE

The priceless gift of life is love,
For with the help of God above,
Love can change the human race
And make this world a better place.

This is the message you heard from the beginning:
We should love one another.
1 JOHN 3:11 NIV

What can you do to uplift the frazzled
salesclerks and others around you?

Love really can change the human race, Father.
I've witnessed it in my circle of friends and loved
ones. Even the most difficult person can be won over
by love. During the Christmas season, may I be
reminded each day of the opportunity You're giving
me to love others as You love me. It's the perfect
time of year to shine with love for You! Amen.

Day 350

UNSELFISH GIVING

If we lived Christmas each
day as we should,
And made it our aim to always do good,
We'd find the lost key to
meaningful living
That comes not from getting,
but from unselfish giving.

He is ever giving liberally and lending,
and his children become a blessing.
PSALM 37:26

What is the difference between happiness and joy?

I love Christmas so much, Lord. There are
times when I would like to celebrate 365 days
a year! Only during the Christmas season does
mankind really come together in harmony,
celebrating the story of Your Son's birth. Oh,
to have this joy every day of the year, Father.
What an amazing way to live! Amen.

NEW HOPE

Just like the seasons that come and go
When the flowers of spring
lie buried in snow,
God sends to the heart
in its winter of sadness
A springtime awakening of
new hope and gladness.

"And now, Lord, for what do I wait?
My hope is in thee."
PSALM 39:7

What daily occurrences give you hope? How can you
share this hope with someone who needs it?

No matter what physical season we're walking
through, Lord—be it winter, spring, summer,
or fall—my heart is alive in You. You can awaken
hope in my soul, even during the coldest, dreariest
times. My hope is always alive, because You are
my hope, Father. Today I choose to live it out
with everyone I come in contact with. Amen.

Day 352

THE CHRISTMAS STAR

It matters not who or what you are;
All men can behold the Christmas Star.
For the Star that shone is shining still
In the hearts of men of peace and goodwill.

*Cast me not away from thy presence, and take not
thy holy Spirit from me. Restore to me the joy of thy
salvation, and uphold me with a willing spirit.*
PSALM 51:11–12

How can you show not only the Christmas spirit but
the Christian spirit to those with whom you come in
contact this month?

---

*Christmas is the season of goodwill, Father!
I love it, because people radiate such joy and
peace through the holidays. You make Yourself
so real to us during the Christmas season, and
people of all faiths are drawn in. Your presence
is undeniable. It changes us for the better.
Thank You for Christmas, Lord. Amen.*

GLAD TIDINGS

In the glad tidings
Of the first Christmas night,
God showed us
The way and the truth and the light.

*Oh send out thy light and thy truth; let them lead me, let
them bring me to thy holy hill and to thy dwelling!*
PSALM 43:3

How can you show others the
way in truth and light today?

---

*I'm trying to imagine what it must have been
like, Lord, to be roused by a heavenly, angelic
choir singing, "Glory to God in the highest!"
How those shepherds must've quivered and
quaked! And yet, how they must have bowed
in awe, hours later, when they approached the
babe in the manger. Coming face-to-face with
the King of kings brings everything into
perspective! What a blessing! Amen.*

Day 354

HEART AWAKENING

Give us faith to believe again
That peace on earth, goodwill to men
Will follow this winter of man's mind
And awaken his heart and make him kind.

And let us not grow weary in well-doing, for in
due season we shall reap, if we do not lose heart.
GALATIANS 6:9

Does your heart need awakening today?
Ask Jesus to give you a spiritual awakening.

Lord, I often wonder if peace on earth is
truly possible. I sometimes doubt that billions
of people with thousands of different ideologies
will ever learn to fully live in harmony. Today,
renew my hope for peace on earth. As I shine my
light for You, Lord, may I point to the Author
of everlasting peace. May I be a goodwill
ambassador for You. Amen.

HUMBLE CHRIST CHILD

God, make us aware that in Thy name
The holy Christ child humbly came
To live on earth and leave behind
New faith and hope for all mankind.

I wait for the Lord, my soul waits,
and in his word I hope.
PSALM 130:5

Imagine being one of the magi.
What would you have said to the baby
Jesus when you first met Him?

Father, I love the story of the magi, who
traveled such a great distance to see baby Jesus
face-to-face. How they must have marveled at
His presence, Lord. How we still marvel at
Your presence! When we enter into the Holy of
Holies with You, we are overwhelmed with faith.
Troubles vanish. Hope is restored. Oh, for just
a moment with You today, Lord. Amen.

Day 356

THE CHRISTMAS PATTERN

The gifts that we give have no purpose
Unless God is part of the giving,
And unless we make Christmas a pattern
To be followed in everyday living.

A man's gift makes room for him
and brings him before great men.
PROVERBS 18:16

What characteristics of Christmas
can you adopt throughout the year?

I love giving gifts at Christmastime, Lord. Doing so
brings great joy and reminds me of the gift You gave
when You sent Your Son for my ransom. May I learn
to make giving a pattern in my life, Father. May I
be known to others as a giver in everyday living.
I want to bless others abundantly, Lord. Amen.

Day 357

SALVATION

Christmas to me
Is a gift from above—
A gift of salvation
Born of God's love.

Steadfast love and faithfulness will meet;
righteousness and peace will kiss each other.
PSALM 85:10

What does Christmas mean to you?

I love the word salvation, *Father! You've*
saved me, redeemed me, brought me back from
the grave. You've ransomed my soul, delivered me
from darkness, set my feet on an eternal path.
What a blessed gift this salvation is! I did nothing
to deserve it, and yet You freely gave Your Son.
I'm eternally grateful, Father. Amen.

MORE THAN A SEASON

Christmas is more than a
day at the end of the year,
More than a season of
joy and good cheer,
Christmas is really God's
pattern for living
To be followed all year
by unselfish giving.

I give thee thanks, O LORD, with my whole heart.
PSALM 138:1

Do you make it a habit to give all year long?
To whom do you give? What causes
are closest to your heart?

---

*Oh, to have the heart of Christmas all year long,
Lord. Looking forward with anticipation to
sharing the story of the baby Jesus. Singing
Christmas carols at the top of our lungs. Tying
up special gifts with ribbons and bows. Sharing
the joy of the season with those we love. Oh, to
live this way 365 days a year, Father! Amen.*

INFINITE LIVING

Christmas is more
Than getting and giving—
It's the why and the wherefore
Of infinite living.

*"Therefore I command you, You shall open
wide your hand to your brother, to the
needy and to the poor, in the land."*
DEUTERONOMY 15:11

Can you help at a homeless shelter or soup
kitchen or donate to a food bank this month?

---

*I've learned eternal truths from the Christmas
story, Father. May I be a giver, not a taker.
May I leave my tasks, as the shepherds did,
to rush to Your side. May I sing, "Glory to God
in the highest!" with the angels and trust You
with quiet strength as Mary did. Most of all,
may I walk with You all the days of my life, Lord,
growing closer to You with each passing day. Amen.*

THE MIRACLE OF CHRISTMAS

Miracles are marvels
That defy all explanation,
And Christmas is a miracle
And not just a celebration.

*I will give to the LORD the thanks due to
his righteousness, and I will sing praise
to the name of the LORD, the Most High.*
PSALM 7:17

When have you witnessed or heard of a
modern-day miracle? What was it?

---

*May we never forget, Lord, what a miracle
Christmas is. Everything about it is supernatural,
from the way Mary learned she was expecting to
the angelic visitation on that holy night. What other
story features a baby—fully God, fully man? What
other tale shares truths that will change eternity?
You're the best Storyteller of all, Father. We praise
You for the Christmas story! Amen.*

KEEP CHRIST IN CHRISTMAS

By keeping Christ in Christmas
We are helping to fulfill
The glad tidings of the angels—
"Peace on earth and to men, goodwill."

Let me hear what God the LORD will speak,
for he will speak peace to his people, to his saints,
to those who turn to him in their hearts.
PSALM 85:8

How do you keep Christ in Christmas?
How can you encourage others to do the same?

You are at the heart of Christmas, Lord!
Without You, there's nothing to celebrate.
May we never forget—amid the presents, food,
and songs—that a Christ-less Christmas is no
Christmas at all. The true story of the Christ child
changed everything. May You always have
Your rightful place, Lord Jesus! Amen.

COMMON GROUND

Peace on earth cannot be found
Until we meet on common ground
And every man becomes a brother
Who worships God and loves all others.

Beloved, if God so loved us,
we also ought to love one another.
1 JOHN 4:11

Do you consider your love for your brothers and
sisters to be a form of worship? Why or why not?

There are so many people across this planet, Lord.
I'll only meet a handful during my lifetime. Many
will be very different from me. Show me how to
extend the hand of friendship to all, regardless of
race, creed, or religion. May I exhibit Christlike
friendship—brotherly love—by opening my hand
and heart to all of Your creation. Amen.

EVERY GOOD GIFT

The richest gifts are God's to give,
May you possess them as long as you live.

Every good endowment and every perfect gift is from
above, coming down from the Father of lights with whom
there is no variation or shadow due to change.
JAMES 1:17

What are some of God's richest gifts?
Which of these have you received?

Father, as we wrap up the Christmas season, I'm
reminded of all of the good gifts You've given me.
They top anything I could wrap up in shiny paper.
Health. Provision. Relationships. Joy. Fellowship.
These are just a few of Your wonderful gifts, Lord.
I'm so overwhelmed at Your generosity, Father.
Thank You for pouring out Your love on me, not just
during the Christmas season, but year-round. Amen.

Day 364

LISTEN

Above the noise and laughter
That is empty, cruel, and loud,
Do you listen for the voice of God
In the restless surging crowd?

God is our refuge and strength,
a very present help in trouble.
PSALM 46:1

Does God have to get your attention with a
deafening noise—or can He do it with a whisper?

I'm listening closely, Lord. As this year draws to a
close and another begins, I know You have exciting
opportunities waiting for me. I don't want to miss
a thing. So, I'll stay tuned in to You, Father, ready
to hear Your voice and follow where You lead.
Thank You for speaking to me and guiding me
to the new stage of my journey. Amen.

Day 365

YEAR-END BLESSINGS

Thank You, dear God,
for the year that now ends
And for the great blessing
of loved ones and friends.

Thou crownest the year with thy bounty.
PSALM 65:11

What has God taught you about yourself this year?
What have you learned about Him?

---

*What an amazing year, Lord! I've grown
in faith and am becoming stronger every day.
I can't wait to see what the new year holds.
What adventures do You have for me, Father?
Will there be exciting new roads to travel? With
Your hand in mine, I can't wait to find out. I praise
You for an exciting journey ahead, Lord. Amen.*

Scripture Index

OLD TESTAMENT

NEW TESTAMENT